PETER 3 PAUL. 2004.

Greenhill Books

MODERN MACHINE-GUNS

GREENHILL MILITARY MANUALS

MODERN MACHINE-GUNS

GREENHILL MILITARY MANUALS

John Walter

Greenhill Books, London
Stackpole Books, Pennsylvania

Greenhill Books

Dedication
To ARW and ADW, with love

Modern Machine-Guns first published 2000 by
Greenhill Books, Lionel Leventhal Limited, Park House, 1 Russell Gardens, London NW11 9NN
and
Stackpole Books, 5067 Ritter Road, Mechanicsburg, PA 17055, USA

British Library Cataloguing in Publication Data
Walter, John, 1951-
Modern machine guns. - (Greenhill military manuals)
1.Machine guns - History
I.Title
355.8'2424

ISBN 1-85367-395-1

Library of Congress Cataloging-in-Publication Data
Walter, John.
Modern machine guns / by John Walter.
p.   cm. -- (Greenhill military manuals)
ISBN 1-85367-395-1
1. Machine guns. I. Title. II. Series. III. Greenhill military manuals.
UF620.A2 W.35 2000   00-021957

Design and layout by John Anastasio, Creative Line
Printed and bound in Singapore by Kyodo Printing Company

Contents

Acknowledgements

Once again, I would like to acknowledge the assistance of Ian Hogg, who very kindly supplied photographs and encouragement, and the help provided by many of the machine-gun manufacturers. The thousands of words written about machine-guns since the end of the Second World War have also been instructive – in particular, books such as *Small Arms of the World* (by W.H.B. Smith, Joseph E. Smith and latterly Edward C. Ezell, all regrettably now dead), and *Military Small Arms of the Twentieth Century* by Ian Hogg and John Weeks. Each of these books has successfully progressed through many editions since first publication in 1960 and 1971 respectively.

Jane's Infantry Weapons, published annually, is also an invaluable source of data, as are the magazines that cater for the defence industries. Edward C. Ezell's *Small Arms Today* provides a painstaking listing of modern military matériel on a country-by-country basis, and the many studies on individual topics – such as Dolph Gaines' trilogy about the Maxim and Vickers Guns, and Musgrave & Oliver's *German Machine Guns* – often fill vital gaps.

I must again thank Alison and Adam, who have accepted books, manuals, photographs and advertising literature strewn across the lounge floor with only an occasional look of exasperation. I'm sure they hope my attention never turns to anything larger than a machine-gun...

John Walter
Hove, 2000

INTRODUCTION

This book contains details of machine-guns ranging from light-support weapons (LSW) and squad automatic weapons (SAW) to general-purpose machine-guns (GPMG), sustained-fire machine-guns (SFMG) and large-calibre guns used in heavy-support and anti-matériel roles. It is often difficult to draw a line between heavy automatic rifles and the lightest of the machine-guns: the Soviet RPK, for example, is simply a heavy-barrelled Kalashnikov automatic rifle.

For the purposes of this particular book, therefore, inclusion as a 'machine-gun' depends on whether the gun can feed ammunition belts, whether the barrel is readily detachable (enabling fire to be sustained), and whether the action fires automatically from the open-bolt position to prevent the effects of barrel heating 'cooking-off' a chambered round before it can be struck by the firing pin. Any gun that fails to satisfy at least one of these three criteria has been considered as a heavy rifle, and relegated to the appropriate book!

The idea of replacing large numbers of men with a single weapon has fascinated designers for many years, credit for the rediscovery of the ancient *ribauldequin* (multi-barrel volley gun from the fifteenth century) now being given largely to a Belgian artilleryman named Fafschamps. In the mid-1860s, the Fafschamps gun was refined for production by Josef Montigny and Louis Christophe; made in Montigny's factory in Fontaine l'Évêque, near Liège, the 37-barrel Mitrailleuse was extensively employed in Belgian strongpoints and, in its improved De Reyffe form, would have served the French well during the Franco-Prussian War had they been prepared to use it properly.

The American Civil War was the first to see the use of *mechanically* operated machine-guns, though doubt remains over the introduction of the first such gun

A Royal Navy machine-gun crew poses with its ten-barrel Gatling Gun, c. 1890. Note that the Number Two in the centre has his right hand on the crank, whilst the Number One, the gun commander, aims the gun from his seat on the trail. This particular gun is fitted with a Broadwell drum magazine. The man behind the gun trail is holding a spare magazine.

in combat, the Confederate Williams Gun and the Union Repeating Gun entering the fray virtually simultaneously.

The best-known of the American Civil War guns is unquestionably the Gatling, patented in 1862, which fired standard combustible cartridges inserted in integrally capped carriers. Gatlings fired several times for each turn of a crank handle on the rear right side of the frame, the striker running through each breechblock being released when it reached a predetermined position.

Mechanical operation

The first Gatlings leaked gas badly and the method of wedging the cartridge-carriers into the breech made the handle difficult to turn. By the middle of the war, however, copper-case cartridges were being used in separate cylindrical inserts – which cured the gas leaks, though accuracy remained poor until the advent of better ammunition. Successful trials had been undertaken in many countries by the early 1870s and Gatling's fortune was assured: guns had been sold to France, Prussia and Japan, and a production licence had been granted to Sir W.G. Armstrong & Co. Ltd in Britain.

Others followed where Gatling led, but only Hotchkiss, Gardner and Nordenfelt experienced any real success. Even then, few designs offered much improvement on the Gatling and, as late

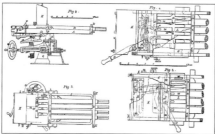

A ten-barrel Nordenfelt gun on a wheeled land carriage and detail drawings of the mechanism. From Engineering, *February and January 1883.*

as 1907-09, M1903 guns were converted by Colt and Springfield Armory to chamber the .30-06 cartridge. Gatlings were finally declared obsolescent in the US Army in 1912, but were discarded only after the end of the First World War. The crank-operated Hotchkiss machine-

gun was essentially similar to the Gatling, though a patent-infringement lawsuit brought by the latter failed. The Hotchkiss was generally made in the form of a large-calibre cannon.

Financed by Thorsten Nordenfelt, whose name they took, the Nordenfelt Guns were designed by a Swedish engineer named Heldge Palmcrantz. The parts were originally made in a factory in Carlsvik, near Stockholm, though many of the guns were assembled in Britain. The Palmcrantz action relied on a reciprocating handle rather than a rotary crank, claimed as a great advantage by champions of the Nordenfelt Gun, but often derided by detractors. Retracting the operating handle first moved the action block laterally to the left, then withdrew the breech pieces through the displaced action block.

The Gardner Gun was patented in the USA in 1874 by William Gardner of Toledo, Ohio. Each of its fixed barrels was accompanied by a reciprocating breechblock driven by a rotary crank. Careful attention to development gradually increased the rate of fire of the mechanism until some of the barrels could be discarded, though Gardners with as many as ten barrels were made for trials.

An idea of the performance of these early 'machine-guns' can be gained by the results of trials undertaken in

Washington Navy Yard in June 1879, where a Gardner Gun fired 6631 rounds in a little under 19 minutes. Six stoppages were caused by a burr on an extractor pawl, but the bolt was then modified and 10,000 rounds were fired in 27½ minutes without a single jam. Yet manually operated guns were doomed by the appearance of the first Maxim Gun. It was soon obvious to all but their most diehard supporters that the mechanically operated machine-gun was inferior to the true automatic.

Maxim and his legacy

The Maxim Gun Company was formed in 1884 to exploit the patents granted to an American, Hiram S. Maxim. A factory was established at Crayford, in Kent, and guns were successfully demonstrated in Britain in November 1885. One of the most impressive exhibitions was held in Vienna in the summer of 1888, where one gun underwent a 13,500-round endurance trial. Apart from the failure of the main spring after 7281 rounds, and a striker breakage at 10,233, few problems were encountered.

The earliest Maxims comprised two basic assemblies. The fixed part was mounted on trunnions. The aiming handles and the trigger lever were attached to this breech-casing. The recoiling assembly slid inside the breech

Swiss cavalrymen attending an armourers' course in 1916 pose with two Maxim machine-guns in front of the Eidgenössische Waffenfabrik, Bern.

casing, moving back through a distance of about an inch. The recoil force was absorbed largely by the spiral main

A selection of weapons is demonstrated to the Chinese Ambassador to Britain by representatives of the Maxim-Nordenfelt Guns & Ammunition Company. Hiram Maxim (in top hat) stands directly to the ambassador's left. In addition to two breech-loading field guns, an assortment of automatic Maxim and manually operated Maxim-Nordenfelt machine-guns may be seen.

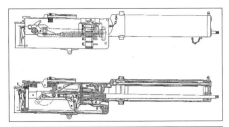

Top *A longitudinal section of a Maxim machine-gun, from a German handbook of 1905.* **Above** *The Soviet PM, still in mass production as late as 1944, typified the Maxim Guns introduced prior to the First World War.*

spring, though a small portion rotated and cocked the hammer.

Though Maxims had been adopted for British service, they were still in short supply when the Second South African War began in 1899. This was typical of the low esteem in which the military authorities of the day viewed the automatic machine-gun. Despite the evidence of the Russo-Japanese War

(where sixteen Russian Maxims had fired nearly 200,000 rounds in a single incident with no mechanical failures), few war departments took much notice. In the decade prior to the beginning of the First World War, British purchases from Vickers, Sons & Maxim and its successor, Vickers Ltd, amounted to a paltry 108 guns.

The advent of the Maxim eclipsed the manually operated multi-barrel gun invented in the 1870s by Benjamin Berkeley Hotchkiss. Hotchkiss et Cie was then approached by an Austrian inventor, Adolf von Odkolek, who had been unable to arouse interest in his flap-locked gas-operated machine-gun. The Hotchkiss management immediately saw the potential of the Odkolek gun, acquiring rights on the harshest possible terms.

By the mid-1890s, the Odkolek had become the Hotchkiss and the inventor was all but forgotten. Pre-1914 machine-guns of this type all fed from distinctive metal strips. They had been tested by the French Army in 1897, upgraded to become the *Modèle* 00 (Mle 00), but then 'improved' by government technicians to become the Mle 05 (Puteaux) and Mle 07 (Saint-Étienne). Fate decreed that Hotchkiss should laugh last: neither of the 'improved' guns was successful and, as short of machine-guns as the British had been when the First World War began, the French authorities sheepishly

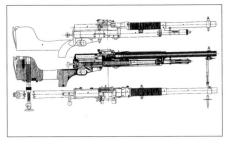

Top *The Hotchkiss light machine-gun or 'machine rifle', characterised by a rigid-strip feed in a misguided quest for efficiency, was popular prior to 1918. From an original pre-1914 handbook.* **Above** *The 7.7mm Japanese Type 92 (1932), with the tripod adapted so that the entire gun could be picked up and moved by three men, was a perfected form of the Hotchkiss.*

ordered huge quantities of weapons from Hotchkiss to supplement the Saint-Étienne.

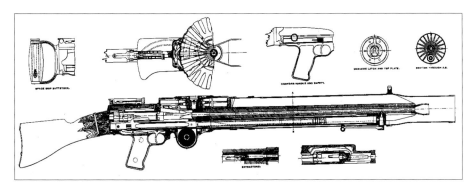

A longitudinal section of a Lewis Gun, from Trade Handbook, Edition No. 4, Lewis Gun *(1914).*

Light machine-guns

Société Française d'Armes Portatives Hotchkiss had also made the *Fusil-Mitrailleur* Mle 09, designed by Laurence Benét and Henri Mercié, which relied on a locking collar containing an interrupted screw; the earlier Odkolek-type Hotchkiss guns had all embodied a flap-lock. In addition, the feed was altered – so that the cartridges lay beneath, instead of above, the flat metal plate that carried them. This made the 1909-type feed-strips much more difficult to load, so awkward, indeed, that rumours abounded in the USA that the 'Machine Gun Rifle, Caliber .30, Model of 1909' could only be fired in daylight!

The concept of machine-rifles intrigued many designers prior to the First World War, but few had been tested successfully. An exception to this rule proved to be the gun developed by a retired American Army officer, Isaac Newton Lewis, on the basis of an unsuccessful weapon designed in 1906–09 by Samuel McClean. McClean's patents had been acquired by the Automatic Arms Company of Buffalo, New York State, and Lewis had been hired to refine the design. Several guns were exhibited at Fort Myers in 1911, but revealed a harsh action and poor extraction.

Lewis and his backers persevered and, by 1913, had persuaded the Belgian Army to adopt their light machine-gun. During the First World War, BSA-made and Savage-made Lewis Guns were impressed into British service in huge numbers. The US Army bought a few hundred .303 Lewis Guns from Savage in 1916 for use in the border wars with Mexico, but a .30-calibre derivative failed largely because the American round was much more powerful than its British equivalent.

The perfected gas-operated Lewis had a rotating pan magazine above the receiver and relied on a turning bolt to lock the action. After the gun fired, gas was tapped off the barrel and led back to

The Lewis was the most successful of the light-support machine-guns issued during the First World War, nearly 150,000 being made in Britain alone. Pictured in the 1920s, these British soldiers pose with their marksmanship trophy. Their silver cup gives scale to the Lewis Gun in the foreground.

11

The .303 Vickers Gun, derived from the Maxim, was the principal British heavy-support machine-gun prior to 1945. Taken on the Western Front in 1917, this picture – obviously posed – shows a gun crew 'in action'. The backsight is down and it seems unlikely that there are cartridges in the feedway.

push the piston rearward. This retracted the striker and revolved the bolt lugs out of engagement with the receiver walls. A large helical spring in a prominent housing beneath the receiver, ahead of the trigger, returned the piston/bolt assembly to battery, and the gun continued to fire as long as the trigger was pressed.

Days of reckoning

By 1914, the machine-gun was established as an efficient weapon and the Maxim and its near-relation, the British Vickers Gun, were serving armies throughout the world. However, many high-ranking soldiers believed that the machine-gun had no place in a 'civilised' war: that such weapons were good only for slaughtering poorly armed natives and that well-trained cavalrymen would simply ride the gunners down. However, the lessons that should have been learned during the Russo-Japanese war of 1904–05 became crystal clear as soon as the First World War had begun. Yet generals still exposed men to death unnecessarily: during the Battle of Loos in 1915, for example, in little more than an hour, German Maxims reduced a twelve-battalion British assault to less than a fifth of its initial strength of about 10,000 men.

When the USA declared war on Germany and its allies, an inventory taken on 6 April 1917 amounted to a mere 670 Benét-Mercié machine-rifles, 282 Maxims, 143 Colt 'Potato Diggers' and 353 Lewis Guns. The situation was eased with the advent of a recoil-operated, water-cooled gun developed by John Browning on the basis of patents dating back to 1901. Performance of the carefully made, belt-feed Browning tested in May 1917 was sensational: 20,000 rounds at a rate of 600 per minute without a failure, then 20,000 more.

Browning then produced a second gun, which was fired continuously for a little over 48 minutes, firing 28,920 shots until all

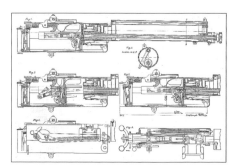

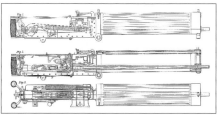

*Longitudinal sections of the Maxim **top** and Vickers **bottom**, showing how the inversion of the toggle lock allowed the depth of the receiver to be reduced. From* Engineering, *January 1907 and April 1911.*

readily available ammunition had been expended. By the end of the test period, one of the guns had fired 396,000 rounds. As the Browning was simpler to make than a Vickers or Hotchkiss equivalent, it was ordered straight into mass production. When assembly finally ceased in 1919, nearly 70,000 Brownings had been made by Colt, Remington and Westinghouse.

An alternative solution to the concept of a light-support weapon was provided by John Browning, who developed the Browning Automatic Rifle (BAR) in 1917. This photograph shows Lieutenant Val Browning, John's nephew, shouldering a prototype.

Technological advances made in the years between the world wars encouraged the development of special-purpose machine-guns. This .303 Vickers K, with a pan magazine, is serving as an observer's gun.

The inter-war period also saw a rise in enthusiasm for the Einheitsmaschinen-gewehr (universal machine-gun) concept mooted during the First World War. This German MG 34, on its tripod, is set for anti-aircraft fire.

Reassessment

The First World War demonstrated the value of the machine-gun in many different roles; comparatively slow-firing guns were ideal for land warfare, but the water-cooled patterns mounted on the tripods necessary to sustain fire effectively were supplemented with lightweight, air-cooled guns providing close-range fire support wherever it was needed.

Each class had its drawbacks. For example, the water in the cooling jacket of the Maxims and similar support weapons began to boil after fire had been sustained at a rate of 200–250rpm for 3 minutes. Steam could be led off through a hose into a condenser can, allowing coolant to be returned to the jacket as required, but there were many times when water ran short and barrels overheated.

Barrel changing could also be unnecessarily complicated. The barrel of the Vickers Gun – typical of its genre – could be changed only by elevating the gun and pulling the barrel back far enough to allow a large cork to be inserted in the aperture in the front of the barrel jacket. The gun was then 13

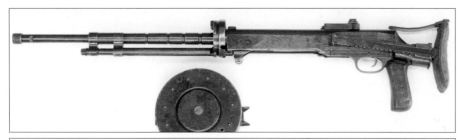

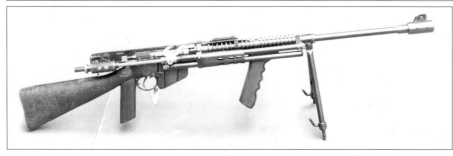

Top Introduced in 1929, the Soviet 7.62mm DT was a minor variant of the standard infantry weapon, the DP, with a pistol grip, a retractable butt and a compact two-tier drum magazine. Another derivative, the DA, was mounted in aircraft. *Centre* A short-barrel MG 34S on a bipod for use in a light-support role. *Bottom* Machine-guns have often been in short supply when wars begin and the Second World War was no exception. This conversion, developed in New Zealand during the Japanese invasion scares of 1942–3, was based on an obsolescent .303 LLE (Lee-Enfield) rifle.

depressed and the barrel could be withdrawn backward. Asbestos string wrapped in grooves in the new barrel acted as a seal; the barrel was simply pushed forward into place, knocking the cork out as it did so. Water was allowed to drain from the bore by depressing the gun, and another 10,000 rounds could be fired before the next change.

Light machine-guns had problems of their own. These were largely due to the barrels, which heated rapidly if fire was sustained for more than a few minutes. One solution was to increase the amount of metal in the barrel simply by making it thicker, adding an unwanted penalty in the form of additional weight, or by increasing the surface area of the barrel by adding circumferential ribs or fins.

The current generation of infantry-support guns is typified by the US M60 which, though belt fed, is light enough to be fired from the hip. One of the biggest drawbacks of the original version was the attachment of the bipod to the barrel unit, which made barrel-changing difficult.

Neither of these was anything more than a compromise and the Germans preferred the MG 08/15, a bipod-mounted light machine-gun with a water-jacketed barrel.

The British Lewis Gun incorporated an innovative 'forced-draught' system, relying on a barrel encased in a ribbed aluminium radiator which was itself inserted in a plain cylindrical jacket. The mouth of the jacket, which was partially open, projected in front of the muzzle. Expansion of propellant gases at the muzzle was supposed to draw air in from the rear of the radiator, along the ribs and out of the muzzle opening.

Machine-guns were adapted during the First World War for aerial use, the advent of hydraulic or mechanical synchronising equipment allowing them to fire through propeller arcs. Some were adapted for use in the earliest tanks, or to provide high-angle anti-aircraft fire. Enterprising designers sought to provide exceptionally high rates of fire, which were proving to be very useful in the air where targets were glimpsed only fleetingly. In Germany, Carl Gast produced a twin-barrel gun with cross-connected breech mechanism and the Hungarian Ferencz Gebauer provided a gun driven directly from the crankshaft of an aero-engine.

The end of the First World War, supposedly the precursor of everlasting peace, presented most armed forces with paradoxical arguments. The reduction of army establishments to a fraction of their wartime strengths led to the scrapping of thousands of guns, yet the emergence of new types of firearm could not be ignored. Among the most important new infantry small arms were the 'machine pistol' (submachine-gun) and the light machine-gun, and most military agencies were well aware that development work was needed to keep abreast of their rivals.

Consequently, the period between the wars was a contrast of great experimentation set against such severe budgetary restrictions that many

*Machine-gun design has always been fluid: tactical needs are constantly reassessed and advances in manufacturing technology inevitably make an impact of their own. Many armies now issue heavy automatic rifles in the guise of light-support weapons (LSW), even though their capacity to sustain fire may be limited by fixed barrels and box magazines. Typical of this genre are the traditionally made 7.62mm FALO, shown below in its Argentine-made version **top**; the 5.56mm Colt M16A2 **centre**; and the Finnish 7.62mm M76 Kalashnikov **bottom**.*

The Ford Aerospace XM248 was an unsuccessful competitor in the US Squad Automatic Weapon trials, won by the Belgian FN XM249 Minimi.

promising designs were stillborn. Much effort was devoted to the development of high-speed aircraft guns (an area in which the Russians, perhaps surprisingly, excelled) and the consequences of the introduction of light machine-guns such as the Czechoslovakian ZB 26 and its derivative, the Bren Gun, are still evident today. The concept of the *Einheitsmaschinengewehr* or 'universal machine-gun', mooted in Germany during the First World War, led to the first generation of multi-purpose gun-systems exemplified by the German MG 34 – which could be issued as easily with a bipod as on a sophisticated buffered-cradle tripod.

It has often been said that more progress is made in a year of war than a decade of peace. This was demonstrated again during the Second World War (1939–45), where the development

of machine-guns that had proceeded

erratically throughout the 1920s and 1930s was given a sharp focus. The goals remained simplicity, reliability and durability, but the large-scale use of armoured vehicles and high-speed aircraft, to name but two of the many factors, influenced designs in ways which had not always been foreseen.

The loss of inventory and manufacturing facilities forced countries such as the USSR and even post-Dunkirk Britain to investigate simplified designs, though, ironically perhaps, the greatest steps forward were made in technologically sophisticated Germany. The Germans were the first to investigate the large-scale use of stampings and pressings, techniques which were used to great effect with the MG 42 – a gun whose lineage may still be seen in the current MG 3 and a whole range of guns made by SIG in Switzerland. Surprisingly crude by the standards of its predecessor, the traditionally made MG 34, the MG 42 proved to be much more reliable. And its unusually high rate of fire made an indelible impression on those who faced it.

The Browning machine-gun is another to have proved its pedigree beyond doubt. Though its high public profile is largely due to the use of .303 Brownings by Spitfire and Hurricane fighters during the Second World War, the .50-calibre version has had the most

significant impact on machine-gun history. Made in huge quantities, mounted on vehicles as well as US aircraft such as the B-17 Flying Fortress and the P-51 Mustang, the .50 Browning remains the machine-gun against which all new designs are measured: light enough to serve in a ground role,

The Belgian-designed 5.56mm Minimi is among the most successful of the current generation of light-support weapons, capable of feeding continuously from a disintegrating-link belt, from a short belt contained in a case, or even from a conventional box magazine.

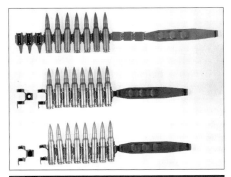

Top Three typical ammunition belts. Top to bottom: the fixed-link German DM1 pattern, shown with the disintegrating-link German DM6 and the disintegrating-link US M13 pattern. *Above* The feedway of the FN Browning M2 HB, showing the belt of .50-calibre cartridges.

powerful enough to defeat even lightly armoured vehicles at moderate range, the Browning still fulfils a valuable role.

One of the most interesting light machine-guns to appear during the Second World War was the American Johnson, fed laterally from a detachable box, but capable of being loaded from conventional rifle-type chargers when required. The barrel was detachable and the gun weighed merely 12.8lb. Though only moderately successful – it was not easy to control – the 1944-type .30-06 Johnson is often considered to be the prototype of the current generation of ultra-lightweight guns.

For all the successes of machine-gun design, there have also been some spectacular failures. One of the silliest episodes was the T24 project, an adaptation of a German MG 42 captured in North Africa for the .30 M1906 cartridge. The Saginaw Steering Gear Division of General Motors supplied two T24 machine-guns, but a 10,000-round endurance trial held at Springfield Armory in February 1944 was suspended after fifty jams in 1483 rounds. Investigation revealed that the designers had failed to allow for the additional length of the .30 M1906 cartridge compared with the German 7.9mm pattern, and the bolt did not recoil far enough. The project was abandoned instead of spending even more money

correcting the flaws.

Springfield Armory reported that the T24 had some excellent features – particularly the barrel-change and the trigger mechanism – but had inadequate reserves of belt-lifting power in adverse conditions and was uncomfortable to fire.

The post-war era has been largely one of consolidation, allowing the best Second World War designs to be honed to perfection alongside others developed to incorporate lessons learned during the fighting. There has been a near-universal reduction in the power of the basic infantry-rifle cartridge, first to the ubiquitous 7.62x51 (.30T65) cartridge, a Winchester design subsequently accepted as NATO standard, then to 5.56x45 (.223); Soviet-bloc armies moved first to 7.62x39, then to 5.45x39.

A steady movement has been made towards light-support or squad automatic weapons, almost always chambering the 5.56mm round; however, these lack the power to provide effective fire-support at ranges beyond 500m and are still supplemented by 7.62mm GPMGs and, when needed, the .50-calibre Brownings. The Soviet bloc has been similarly affected, retaining the venerable rimmed 7.62x54 cartridge for medium-support weapons and the 12.7x108 or 14.5x114 rimless rounds for the NSV and KPV heavy machine-guns.

Only the Belgian FN Minimi has really 17

This folded Steyr-made M74 tripod is typical of the lightweight, but sophisticated, mounts supplied for today's machine-guns.

established itself in the 5.56mm class. Though there has never been a shortage of worthwhile competitors, the acceptance of the Minimi as the standard US Army squad automatic weapon (M249) has been an important catalyst in its success. The Soviet/Russian equivalent is the RPK-74, a heavy-barrelled Kalashnikov assault rifle chambered for the 5.45x39

cartridge, but this lacks the detachable-barrelled Minimi's ability to sustain fire for lengthy periods.

The 7.62mm FN MAG and its derivatives are still the most widely distributed GPMGs, used in more than sixty countries in quantities running into millions; however, the US M60 series and the delayed-blowback Heckler & Koch designs have also proved popular. The standard Soviet/Russian equivalent has been the Kalashnikov-designed PK, an efficient design handicapped by an antiquated rimmed cartridge which must be withdrawn backward from the feed belt before being rammed into the chamber.

Though much development time has been expended on guns such as the FN BRG-15, the proven reliability and 'ex stock' supply of .50-calibre M2 derivatives made by FN Herstal SA and Saco Defense, Inc., ensures that the Brownings are still the most popular in their class. The current Russian equivalent, the 12.7mm NSV, is still rarely seen in the West.

The future

It is hard to see where and how the development of machine-guns will progress, as the genre is still clinging to designs which originated more than fifty years ago. The Brownings were created during the First World War, yet their

efficiency is undisputed and the development of better mountings and control systems has greatly increased their utility. Attempts to provide caseless ammunition seem to have failed and the introduction of proprietary ammunition – always a gamble commercially! – may continue to hamstring potentially world-beating designs.

One major change, however, concerns the renaissance of the externally powered gun. The US Navy experimented with a Gatling Gun powered by a separate Crocker-Wheeler electric motor, reaching 1500rds/min as long ago as 1890. Gatling then integrated the motor drive with the receiver, patenting the design in 1893, and was able to attain a stupendous 3000rds/min.

Demonstrations of the powered Gatlings failed to convince the armies of the day of their value, largely because observers were concerned only with the prodigious usage of ammunition. When aerial warfare began in the First World War, however, the value of ultra-high rates of fire was finally seen. The practicable maximum for a single-barrel gun was established in the 1920s at about 2000rds/min, but only the Soviet ShKAS achieved widespread distribution and then only within the USSR prior to the Spanish Civil War. Most designs were simply much too complicated to be durable, or too weak to withstand the

A 5.56mm XM214 Minigun with a side-stripping or 'delinking' feeder.

altered. Data have been repeated in so many periodicals without critical scrutiny that mistakes become accepted as 'fact' and the truth may be criticised as 'inaccurate'. I have, therefore, given the sources of information, where known with certainty, in individual data tables. Additional details may be found in *The Greenhill Military Small Arms Data Book* by Ian Hogg.

Names of originating countries are given in the form used at the time of a gun's design.

tremendous battering they received from even rifle-calibre ammunition.

In 1944, the US Army experimentally motorised an ancient .45-70 Gatling Gun taken from the Aberdeen Proving Ground Museum and easily reached a fire-rate of 5000rds/min. Encouraged by the performance of an essentially simple weapon, the authorities ordered the Armament Division of General Electric to develop battleworthy designs under the codename 'Vulcan'. The .60-calibre T45 of 1949 led to the improved .60 T62, but work subsequently concentrated on the 20mm M61 – adopted in 1956 – and inspired experimentation that has led to a 'Soviet Gatling' and the Hughes Chain Gun.

The outstanding success of the six- and three-barrel 20mm Vulcans inspired not only the development of 7.62mm and 5.56mm Miniguns in the 1960s, but also the advent of mechanically driven weapons. These have proved to be very effective in airborne gunships, though ground roles are customarily restricted by the availability of sufficient ammunition to sustain fire for longer than a few minutes.

Note on Data

Manufacturers often revise gun specifications during production lives that can stretch over many years. For example, materials may change, features may be added and dimensions can be

OPERATING SYSTEMS

Most of the first successful automatic machine-guns were **recoil operated**, by allowing the parts to move backward – or *recoil* – to open the breech. Among the most successful of the earliest designs were the Maxim and the Vickers Gun, which relied on a toggle lock (not unlike the human knee joint) to form the rigid strut that kept the breech closed until the residual pressure within the cartridge case dropped to a point where the brass walls of the cartridge case were no longer being pressed tightly against the surface of the chamber. This ensured that the spent case would extract satisfactorily as the breech opened. Other guns relied on flap-locks, or on rotating bolts.

Recoil operation falls into two basic categories: *short* and *long* recoil, the arbiter usually being the distance travelled by the locked parts in relation to the length of the cartridge case. Long recoil often involves distances of 75–80mm or more, whereas the locked-breech movement in short recoil designs is rarely more than 15mm.

In the long-recoil system, the bolt is locked to the barrel extension **c** by the locking arm **b** as the gun fires. The barrel and bolt then begin to move back, still securely linked, until the tail of the unlocking bar **d** rides over the bolt latch **f**.

The barrel-return spring **a**, concentric with the barrel, then begins to pull the parts back to battery. However, at position **i**, the unlocking bar is held by the projecting tail of the bolt latch **f** and this in turn pivots the locking arm (at position **g**) to release the barrel and bolt. The barrel runs forward by itself, allowing the extractor in the now static breechblock to withdraw the spent case **h** from the chamber. As the barrel reaches battery (at position **j**), it forces the latch **f** downward and releases the bolt (at position **k**). The bolt-return spring **e** then presses the bolt forward. When the bolt finally catches up with the barrel, the locking arm **b** re-engages with the barrel extension and the gun is locked ready to fire again.

Short recoil is essentially similar, but often entails additional complication. At the instant the gun fires, the bolt is held to the barrel extension by the locking bar **d**. After the parts have moved a short distance backward, a cam surface inside the top plate of the receiver tips the locking bar **d** to break the link between the bolt and the barrel extension. The barrel is halted by a buffer **c** and held in place by the latch **f**. The accelerator **e**, meanwhile, gives additional rearward impetus to the bolt, which continues back alone to extract the spent case.

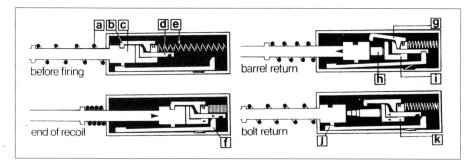

*Long recoil. Key: **a** barrel-return spring, **b** locking arm, **c** barrel extension, **d** unlocking bar, **e** bolt-return spring, **f** bolt latch, **g** lock open, **h** spent cartridge case, **i** bolt latched, **j** lugs re-engaged, **k** bolt unlatched.*

When the bolt has reached the limit of its backward movement, the bolt-return spring **g** reasserts itself and drives the bolt forward once again. As the tail of the bolt passes the projection on the tail of latch **f**, it pivots the latch to release the barrel extension. The barrel-return spring **a** then forces the barrel back to battery, followed by the bolt. A new cartridge is stripped into the chamber, and, often before the components have reached the limit of their forward travel, the locking arm **d** re-engages to allow the gun to fire again.

The principal rival of recoil is **gas operation**, which takes a tiny part of the propellant gas and leads it back to operate a piston. The piston usually lies beneath the barrel, a small port communicating with the bore allowing the gas to bleed out. The position of the port effectively controls the delay before the breech unlocks. Gas-operated guns, theoretically at least, are simpler than recoil-operated equivalents; they are much easier to make, and do not need carefully machined sliding surfaces to operate properly.

Gas operation was inefficient if the ammunition had been loaded with black powder, as the fouling soon clogged the bore, the gas port and the piston chamber. However, the advent of smokeless propellant in the last decade of the nineteenth century – and steady improvement in propellant-making processes – gave an impetus to the development of gas-operated automatic weapons. The Hotchkiss machine-gun was probably the most successful exponent prior to the First World War, but virtually all modern designs operate in this way. Most of the exceptions, such as the Brownings, prove to have originated prior to 1918.

Gas operation is comparatively simple. Part of the propellant gas is tapped from the bore by way of a port, striking the head **a** of a piston before being vented to the atmosphere. The piston, attached to a rod **b** connected to the bolt carrier, pushes backward. This movement has the effect of pulling the locking shoulders on the top surface of the bolt **d** from engagement with recessess **e** in the top of the receiver **c**, thanks to the link between the bolt and

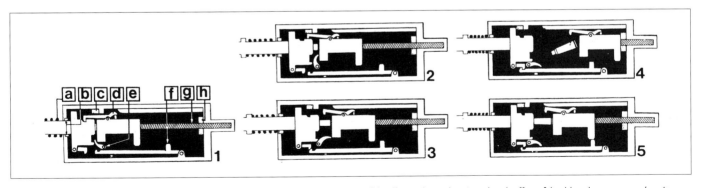

*Short recoil, sequence 1–5. Key: **a** barrel-return spring, **b** counter-recoil buffer, **c** barrel-extension buffer, **d** locking bar, **e** accelerator bar, **f** bolt latch, **g** bolt-return spring, **h** backplate buffer.*

the bolt carrier. The unlocked bolt then continues backward to the limit of its rearward travel, extracting the spent case, until the return spring reasserts itself. The bolt is then propelled forward into battery, stripping a new round into the chamber and the rear cam surfaces of the bolt carrier raise the bolt **d** back into engagement with the receiver recesses **e**.

Other operating methods include **blowback**, which relies on nothing but the inertia of a heavy breechblock, friction between sliding surfaces and the opposition of a powerful spring to delay the opening of the breech; **delayed blowback** adds elements such as swinging levers or multi-part breechblocks to buy a little more time before the

breechblock begins to move back.

Machine-guns which lacked mechanical locking systems were unpopular with military authorities prior to 1945, largely because extraction was almost always harsh. Unless the cartridges were lubricated – manufactured with a wax coating perhaps, or squirted with oil as they entered the chamber – the extractors were prone to tear through the case-rims or even rip the entire case head away, jamming the action.

However, though gas-operated machine-guns are still in the majority, post-1945 views have been altered by the success of delayed blowback roller-locking systems incorporated in Mauser weapons tested experimentally in the closing stages of the Second World War.

Featured more recently in many CETME/Heckler & Koch designs, delayed blowback has achieved belated official approval. The French AAT52 embodies a two-piece bolt and a lever-like 'retarder', and some of the SIG designs also rely on roller delays. Guns of this type now customarily have fluted chambers, effectively floating cartridges on a cushion of gas in an attempt (usually successful) to improve extraction.

Many different feed systems have been tried in machine-guns, including a variety of gravity-fed and spring-fed hoppers, rigid or articulated strips, pans and drums. The most successful post-1945 weapons have almost always relied on box magazines or belt feed, the FN Minimi being one of the few to accept both. Though the essence of belt feed is simple, it is probably true to say that more patents have been sought in this category than for any other facet of machine-gun design, with the possible exception of mountings.

Virtually all feed systems now rely on levers and pawls translating the reciprocating movement of the bolt or breechblock into a lateral cartridge-moving stroke. Most guns rely on a stud on the bolt carrier to raise the belt, though there are exceptions: the Soviet RP-46, for example, had a forked lever oscillated by the movement of the charging handle.

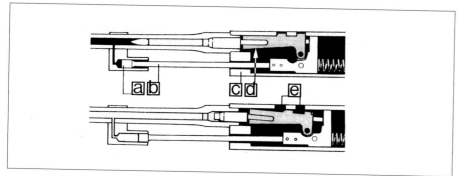

*Gas operation. Key: **a** piston head, **b** piston/operating rod, **c** receiver, **d** bolt, **e** locking recesses.*

Light-support machine-gun
Made by Steyr-Mannlicher GmbH, Steyr
Specification AUG-LMG
Data from Steyr literature, 1987
Calibre 5.56mm (.223)
Cartridge 5.56x45, rimless
Operation Gas operated, selective fire
Locking system Rotating bolt engaging in barrel extension
Length 900mm
Weight 4.03kg with bipod and empty thirty-round magazine
Barrel 621mm, six grooves, right-hand twist
Feed Detachable box magazine with thirty or forty-two rounds
Rate of fire 750±100rds/min
Muzzle velocity 975m/sec (M193 ball ammunition)

This is simply a heavy-barrelled version of the 5.56mm AUG or *Armee-Universal-Gewehr*, Steyr's standard assault rifle. It shares similar futuristic lines, with a large synthetic trigger guard moulded as an integral part of the butt, and retains the folding hand grip on the fore-end. The heavy barrel is not readily exchangeable, but the use of box magazines automatically restricts the effective fire-rate; ten magazines – 300 rounds – can generally be fired continuously.

Unlike the rifle-pattern AUG, the light-support weapon fires automatically from an open bolt. A bipod is fitted to the muzzle, the special muzzle brake/compensator has been developed specifically to reduce the sensation of recoil, and a sturdy 1.5x optical sight is built into the carrying handle.

Variants
AUG-LMG T Identical mechanically with the standard version, this lacks the integral optical sight. Instead, a rail above the receiver will accept any optical, electro-optical or thermal-imaging sight complying with STANAG requirements (NATO military standardisation); Steyr considers a 4x Schmidt & Bender telescope sight to be standard.

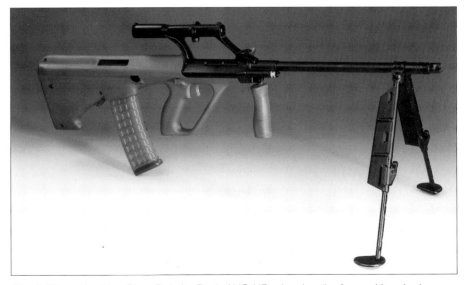

The 5.56mm Austrian Steyr-Daimler-Puch AUG HB, showing the forward hand grip.   **23**

Light-support machine-gun
Made by the Lithgow small arms factory, Lithgow, New South Wales
Specification F89, standard light pattern
Calibre 5.56mm (.223)
Cartridge 5.56x45, rimless
Operation Gas operated, automatic fire only
Locking system Rotating bolt

engaging in receiver
Length 1040mm
Weight 6.9kg with bipod
Barrel 465mm, six grooves, right-hand twist
Feed 200-round metal-link belt or detachable thirty-round box magazine
Rate of fire 500±50rds/min
Muzzle velocity 975m/sec (M193 ball ammunition)

This is little more than a duplicate of the Belgian Minimi (q.v.), with a few changes made to suit Australian production techniques. The dual belt/box-magazine feed system has been retained and the most obvious distinguishing characteristic is the butt – a solid slab-type synthetic component instead of the tube design associated with the Belgian prototype. In this respect, the F89 parallels the US M249.

The 5.56mm Australian F89 machine-gun is a minor variant of the FN Minimi.

Uirapuru   Brazil

*General-purpose, aircraft or vehicle
machine-gun*
Made by Mekanika Indústria e Comércio
Ltda (MIC), Rio de Janeiro
Specification Uirapuru
Calibre 7.62mm (.30)
Cartridge 7.62x51 NATO, rimless
Operation Gas operated, automatic fire
only
Locking system Rotating bolt
Length 1300mm
Weight 13kg (with bipod)
Barrel 600mm, six grooves, right-hand
twist
Feed Metal-link belt

Rate of fire 700±50rds/min
Muzzle velocity 850m/sec

The prototypes of this interesting gun,
designed by a group of technicians
attached to the Brazilian Army's
engineering institute, were test-fired in
1970. However, their performance was
unacceptable and the entire project was
handed over to a member of the original
design group, Olympio Vieira de Mello.
By 1976, Vieira de Mello had refined the
gun sufficiently to impress the army and
– in 1977 – a production licence was
granted to MIC.

The Uirapuru is a distinctive design,
with a slender tubular receiver beneath a
square feed cover. It can be fitted with a
wooden butt and mounted on a bipod to
serve as a light infantry-support gun;
issued on a tripod to enable fire to be
sustained; or mounted coaxially with the
main armament of a tank. The tank gun is
usually fired by a solenoid and may have
a cable-type charging system. Guns
have also been mounted in aircraft and
on patrol boats. The barrel can be
detached in a matter of seconds and, in
its ground roles, has a prominent flash
suppressor/muzzle brake.

Left *The Brazilian 7.62mm Uirapuru GPMG, emphasising the slenderness of its design.* **Right** *The prototype Uirapuru machine-gun
had the carrying handle set at an angle, making it awkward to carry.*

FN MAG series

Belgium

Mitrailleuse d'Appui Générale or Mitrailleuse à Gaz; general-purpose, aircraft or vehicle machine-gun
Made by Fabrique Nationale Herstal SA, Herstal
Specification MAG, light-support version
Calibre 7.62mm (.30)

Cartridge 7.62x51, rimless
Operation Gas operated, automatic fire only
Locking system Displacement of the bolt-tail into the receiver
Length 1260mm
Weight 11kg (with butt and bipod)

Barrel 630mm with flash-hider, four grooves, right-hand twist
Feed Metal-link belt
Rate of fire 800±200rds/min (adjustable)
Muzzle velocity 840m/sec

The FN MAG has proved popular worldwide. This is a tripod-mounted L7A1, made in Britain.

This has been the most successful of all the post-1945 air-cooled medium-support designs. Designed by Ernest Vervier in 1957–8, the prototypes were demonstrated successfully and the MAG has since been sold worldwide in huge quantities: FN alone had sold more than 150,000 by 1979 and many others have been made under licence in Britain, Sweden and the USA.

The key to the success of the MAG lies in its simple tipping-block breech mechanism and the conventionality of its gas-piston system. The smooth-surfaced barrel is heavy enough to withstand continuous firing for some time, but can be detached simply by cocking the gun, applying the safety catch, lifting the top cover if an ammunition belt is still in place, releasing the latch (on the left side of the receiver directly below the carrying handle), and rotating the barrel assembly anti-clockwise until the handle is vertical. The barrel, gas-port block and front-sight assembly can then be drawn forwards.

The standard gun has a sturdy receiver made of heavy-duty forgings and pressings which have been riveted together. The bipod can be folded back under the barrel, providing an acceptable, if rudimentary, fore-end to grip when firing from the hip, and a rotating selector on the gas-port assembly – on the basic Belgian-made version, at least – allows the cyclic rate to be varied from 650rds/min to 1000rds/min.

The feedway can accommodate either German DM1 fixed-link or US M13 disintegrating-link belts; the inner surfaces of the feedway are chromium plated to extend their service lives. The backsight is a folding tangent-leaf pattern on the top rear side of the receiver, graduated from 300m to 800m with the leaf down, relying on the ramp for elevation, and from 800m to 1800m with the leaf upright. The butt is customarily made of wood, with a sling ring formed integrally with the butt plate. Accessories include a webbing holdall with maintenance and cleaning tools; a blank-firing adaptor; webbing covers for the MAG (OREA 681) and its spare barrels (OREA 2660); and a 250-round ammunition box (M61).

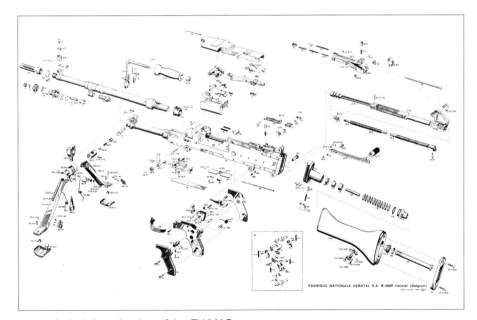

An exploded-view drawing of the FN MAG.

Though usually encountered with a bipod mount, the MAG can also be supplied with the FN 360 Tripod, a special buffered design developed to promote steady and accurate automatic fire. Supplied with a removable bracket for an ammunition box, the mount weighs 11kg and has a maximum base diameter of 1400mm when unfolded. It can be altered to give either infinite adjustment or a three-position 'above ground' gun height of 300mm, 496mm or 600mm, and can give an elevation or depression of 30 degrees (70-degree depression if the two legs are forward). A telescopic anti-aircraft pillar allowing a maximum elevation of 80 degrees can be supplied as an optional extra. Ring-type anti-aircraft sights can be fitted to the fore-end of the gun over the barrel.

Variants
Aircraft version Also known as the Model 60-30 (single mount) or 60-40 (twin mount), this is a straightforward derivative of the standard 60-20 ground gun. Alterations to the feed mechanism allow M13 disintegrating-link belts to be used from either side, and the barrel lacks sights or carrying handle. The butt, bipod, backsight and ejection-port cover are all omitted; the special trigger is customarily operated by a solenoid and an operating loop passing through a hole drilled through the trigger lever; and the

An FN MAG on a pillar mount in a helicopter doorway.

barrel-lock, normally equipped with a spring, is held in place with a screw and safety wire. The charging handle is sometimes replaced with a cable-type retractor.

Coaxial version Often known by the catalogue number 60-40, this is a minor variant of the standard 60-20 pattern, mounted alongside the main turret gun in tanks and armoured vehicles. The barrel lacks sights and carrying handle, ports are eliminated from the gas regulator to prevent exhaust gases entering the vehicle, the bipod and the ejection-port cover are omitted; and the backsight, butt and sling swivels are abandoned. Some guns retain the normal trigger and pistol grip assembly, though others have a special grip cut down to the under-edge of the trigger lever. All vehicle guns, whatever their detail design, can be dismounted and fitted with bipods and butts – carried separately – to serve as rudimentary local-defence weapons.

Top An FN MAG on an anti-aircraft mount, showing the auxiliary ring-and-bead sights.
Above This version of the FN MAG is designed to be mounted coaxially with the main armament of a tank or armoured car. Note the buffer-spring housing protruding from the backplate and the solenoid-type firing system.

Light-support, vehicle or aircraft machine-gun
Made by Fabrique Nationale Herstal SA, Herstal

Specification Minimi
Data for standard model
Calibre 5.56mm (.223)
Cartridge 5.56x45, rimless
Operation Gas operated, selective fire
Locking system Lugs on the bolt rotate into recesses in the barrel extension
Length 1040mm
Weight 6.83kg (with bipod)
Barrel 466mm, six grooves, right-hand twist
Feed 200-round metal-link belt or detachable thirty-round box magazine
Rate of fire 500±50rds/min
Muzzle velocity 925m/sec with SS109 ball ammunition

One of the most successful of the weapons in the light-support category, the Minimi has been adopted worldwide. Among the most important users are the US and Australian armed forces, where it is being used as the M249 and F89 respectively, and copies have been made in several countries (e.g., by Daewoo in Korea).

The 5.56mm FN Minimi is seen as a companion to the FNC (automatic rifle), shown here with their accessories. The machine-gun can feed either from belts or NATO-standard box magazines.

The Minimi was designed as a light-support partner to the 5.56mm FNC automatic rifle and was intended to share a certain commonality of parts. However, owing to changes made since their introduction, the two guns now differ in many respects. Compared with the prototype and pre-production guns, the perfected Minimi has a different butt, with a bent under-tube and a strengthening fillet instead of two straight tubes; an improved backsight, with a windage adjustment protected by longer 'ears' with a distinctive circular void; a ribbed pistol grip instead of a plain-surface pattern; an angular fore-end with integral chequering instead of a rounded pattern with a longitudinal flute; and an improved adjustable three-position bipod with prominent slots in its legs instead of the original plainer four-position type. The bipod can be folded back under the fore-end if the gun is being fired from the hip with the support of a sling or, alternatively, can be folded forward beneath the barrel to allow the gun to be mounted on its tripod.

The Minimi is gas operated, locked by rotating lugs on the bolt into the barrel extension. The barrel unit can be detached in seconds, taking with it the carrying handle, the gas-port block and power adjuster, and the front sight. Most barrels are chromium plated internally to extend their service life. A shoulder

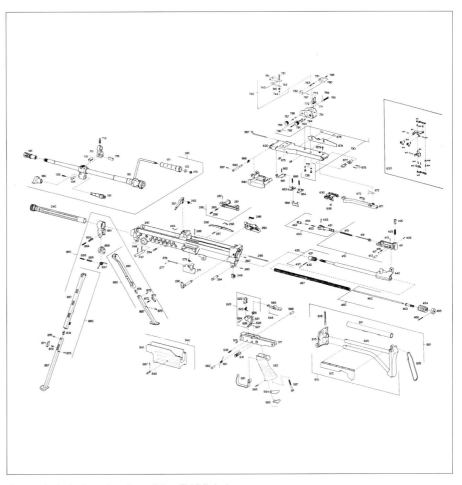

An exploded-view drawing of the FN Minimi.

support is incorporated in the butt plate and the trigger guard can be detached to allow the gun to be used when the firer is wearing arctic mittens.

The most unusual feature of the design, however, lies in its unique dual-feed capabilities. In addition to a conventional disintegrating-link belt, which feeds from the left from a 'hanging belt' or a box attached to the receiver, the Minimi can also fire from standard thirty-round box magazines without requiring adaptation. These are inserted in the feedway on the left side of the receiver, directly below the belt tray, and protrude diagonally. A red-marked blade-type cartridge indicator – visible and tactile – rises from the feed cover when a cartridge is on the feed tray. The sling can be attached to a ring on top of the butt plate and a hole bored transversely through the front-sight block.

A safety catch runs through the receiver immediately above the pistol grip, and a two-position selector lever protruding from the gas-piston block allows the power to be altered to suit

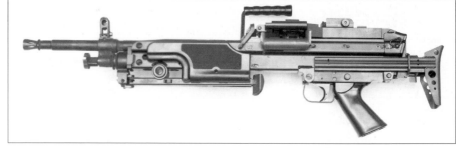

Top right A three-quarters view of the 5.56mm Minimi, showing how the adaptor for the box magazine fits underneath the feedway for the belt.
Right The original 5.56mm FN Minimi-Para had a sliding butt.

ammunition: depending on the rifling, the gun may be adapted for Belgian SS109 or US M193 ball rounds. Like all guns of its type, the Minimi fires from an open breech to minimise cook-off problems, and has a special auxiliary notch in the bolt to prevent the gun running away if the bolt fails to recoil far enough to be caught by the normal sear.

A multi-piece cleaning kit is carried within the detachable fore-end, with an oil bottle in the pistol grip. Accessories include the FN 360 or US M122 tripod, the latter requiring a special adaptor. A blank-firing device can be attached to the muzzle and a rail for optical or electro-optical sights can be attached above the receiver, offset to the left side to clear the backsight protectors.

Variants
Para Model This is a short-barrelled version of the Minimi, intended for paratroops, vehicle-borne personnel and anyone else to whom its compact dimensions appeal. The most obvious characteristics are a reduction in barrel length to merely 347mm, which means

Left *These views of the current Minimi-Para show how the new two-tube butt rotates through 90 degrees, then slides forward alongside the receiver. Note, too, the ultra-short barrel.*

that the flash-hider virtually abuts the gas-port block, and the replacement of the fixed butt. The new butt consists of two parallel struts connected with a butt plate; it turns through 90 degrees to allow the struts to slide forward along the receiver. The Para version is 893mm long with the butt extended, or only 736mm with it retracted; weight averages 6.75kg, muzzle velocity from the short barrel dropping from 925m/sec to about 866m/sec (SS 109 ball rounds).

Vehicle Model This is simply a stripped 466mm-barrelled Minimi with a special buttless backplate. It lacks the bipod and the fixed sights, and is customarily fired by a solenoid in a coaxial mount. Length is merely 793mm, weight being about 5.3kg.

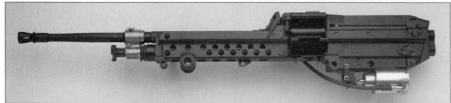

Top The FN 5.56mm Minimi-Para is a very compact design. **Above** The vehicle variant
34 of the 5.56mm Minimi machine-gun, with an electrically operated solenoid trigger system.

FN Browning, .50 series

Heavy-support, vehicle or aircraft machine-gun
Made by Fabrique Nationale Herstal SA, Herstal
Specification FN Browning M2 HB-QCB
Calibre 12.7mm (.50)

Cartridge 12.7x99, rimless
Operation Recoil operated, automatic fire only
Locking system Rising block engages a recess in the bolt
Length 1654mm
Weight 38.15kg (plus 19.95kg for the M3 tripod)

Barrel 1143mm, eight grooves, right-hand twist
Feed Metal-link belt
Rate of fire 450 or 635rds/min
Muzzle velocity 920m/sec with M33 ball ammunition

The current version of the FN-made .50 Browning M2, with quick-change barrel (QCB) and the standard US-pattern tripod.

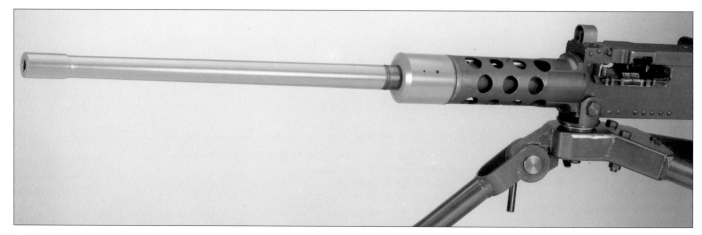

The blank-firing barrel attached to the FN M2 QCB Browning.

This is a minor variant of the original US M2 Browning (q.v.), with changes made to suit European production standards. The guns have deep squared receivers, made of riveted pressings and forgings, with an articulated charging handle and slide assembly on the right side. Belt feed may be from either side. A buffer housing protrudes from the backplate, which also carries the spade grips and the trigger/safety system. The backsight consists of a sight-notch block sliding within a leaf, graduated 100–2600m, under control of an endless screw turned by a knurled drum. The sight leaf pivots within sturdy protectors on top of the rear of the receiver, the front sight being a hooded blade on the front edge of the receiver behind the short barrel-support sleeve. This gives an unusually short sight radius for a gun of the M2 Browning's size, but is entirely adequate for a machine-gun in which dispersion is sometimes as important as single-round accuracy. The barrel sleeve is perforated to encourage the circulation of air necessary to cool the barrel.

The first FN-made guns were practically identical to their American prototypes, complete with the very unsatisfactory method of barrel changing which required care and time to adjust the headspace. However, these were replaced in the 1980s by the M2 HB-QCB, with a quick-change barrel. This can be changed in a few seconds: it is necessary only to retract the charging handle to its rearmost position, rotate the carrying handle to the right to disengage the retaining lug, then pull the barrel forward and out of the barrel-support sleeve. A new barrel can then be inserted and locked in place by turning the carrying handle back leftward to its original position.

Original M2 HB machine-guns can be altered with a special upgrade kit, containing a new barrel, a barrel extension, a breech lock, a shim for the barrel-support sleeve, the barrel-support sleeve itself, and a new accelerator which effectively increases the cyclic rate. Alternatively, old barrels can be modified to save expense. New barrels may have chromed bores and chambers, or the bore may be chromed with a Stellite liner inserted in the mouth of the chamber.

The standard mount is the US tripod, accessories including a special 'booster barrel', which can function either with conventional blanks (with the muzzle plug) or frangible plastic bullets (with the plug removed). SG 127 pedestal and RM 127 ring mounts can be obtained for use in helicopter and gunship doorways or on light warships, while the US M63 quadrupod anti-aircraft mount can also be used – a role in which the optional ring-type anti-aircraft front sight is obligatory.

The standard M3 tripod allows a 45-degree traverse, a maximum elevation of 5.6 degrees, and a depression of 14 degrees. The M63, with a maximum base diameter of 1.32m and all-round traverse, gives an elevation of 85 degrees and a depression of 29 degrees; it weighs about 65.5kg with the gun-cradle.

Variants

M2 HB coaxial This is a simplified form of the standard ground gun, lacking sights. Solenoid or cable-type triggers may be fitted, together with a cable-type charging handle.

M3M Restricted to high-rate (950–1100rds/min) automatic fire, this is a pintle/pillar mount variation of the lightweight M3P described below. The backplate carries spade grips and a conventional trigger button.

M3P A lightweight version of the M2, intended for airborne use in wing- or fuselage-mounted HMPs (Heavy Machine-gun Pods), this has a light barrel, a solenoid firing mechanism and a fired-round counter. It also has a stronger recoil spring to handle the increased cyclic rate (950–1100rds/min) and a buffer housing which protrudes farther from the backplate than normal M2 practice. The full-length barrel jacket may be accompanied by a flash-hider, and an 'anti-cook-off' attachment may also be fitted.

Vickers Gun

Medium-support machine-gun
Made by Vickers Ltd and Vickers-
Armstrong Ltd, Crayford, Kent

Specification Vickers Mk I
Calibre 7.7mm (.303)
Cartridge .303 rimmed (7.7x56)

Operation Recoil operated, automatic
fire only
Locking system Toggle mechanism,

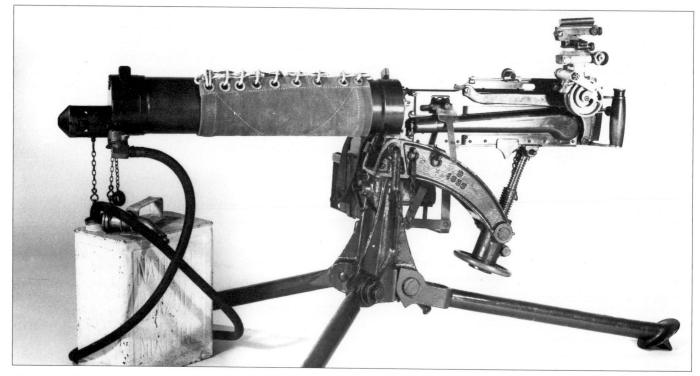

38 *A water-cooled British .303 Mk I Vickers Gun, mounted on a Mk IVB tripod.*

breaking downward
Length 1156mm
Weight 18.15kg with full water jacket
(plus 22.65kg for Mk IV tripod)
Barrel 724mm, five grooves, right-hand
twist
Feed 250-round fabric belt
Rate of fire 450±50rds/min
Muzzle velocity 745m/sec

The 'Gun, Machine, Vickers, .303-inch Mark I' was introduced as long ago as November 1912, a testimony to the efficiency of the basic design. Not declared obsolete until 24 April 1968, the Vickers saw service in all theatres of war, in armoured vehicles and in aircraft.

The Vickers was the outcome of attempts to lighten the Maxim action without sacrificing strength, but remained a 'first generation' weapon: heavy, cumbersome, and comparatively unsophisticated, but sturdy and surprisingly reliable. It was characterised by a deep slab-sided receiver, with spade grips and a thumb trigger mounted on the backplate. A large pivoting bar-type backsight lay on top of the receiver cover. The feed accepted a closed-pocket fabric belt, which fed from the right. One distinguishing feature of both Vickers and Maxim guns was the position of the return spring or fusée beneath a cover on the left side of the receiver.

The Vickers Gun was originally issued with the 'Mounting, Machine-gun, Tripod, Mark IV', which replaced the older Maxim carriages in 1906. The Mark IV was eventually superseded by the essentially similar Mark IVB, the most obvious distinguishing feature being the latter's small traverse ring.

Variants
Most of the .303-calibre aircraft and vehicle guns derived from the Vickers had been declared obsolete by 1945; excepting the Mark III (N), all .5-calibre guns had also been abandoned by this time.

Bren Gun, .303 series

Britain

Light-support machine-gun
Made by the Royal Small Arms Factory, Enfield Lock, Middlesex, and by other contractors (*see* text)
Specification .303 Bren Mk I
Calibre .303 (7.7mm)
Cartridge .303 rimmed (7.7x56mm)

Operation Gas operated, selective fire
Locking system Displacement of the bolt-tail into the receiver
Length 1156mm
Weight 10.52kg with bipod and empty magazine
Barrel 635mm, four grooves, right-

hand twist
Feed Detachable thirty-round box magazine
Rate of fire 540±50rds/min
Muzzle velocity 745m/sec

Marked 'ZGB vz. 33', this Brno-made Bren Gun prototype shows its box magazine to good advantage. The sharp curve of the body was essential to accommodate the rimmed British .303 cartridge.

Derived from the Czechoslovakian vz. 27 (q.v. under ZB vz. 30) by way of the ZGB Models 1–4 of 1931–4, this exceptionally successful weapon was adopted in Britain in May 1935. Though a few 'Guns, Machine, Bren, .303-inch Mark I' were supplied from Brno to enable field trials to be undertaken, the first British-made gun was accepted in September 1937. In October 1938, a supplementary order was given to the John Inglis Company of Toronto, the first Canadian-made Mk I being test-fired in the spring of 1940.

The Bren action relies on cams on an extension of the piston-rod/carrier unit to tilt the back of the breechblock into engagement with the top of the receiver. The half-length gas tube beneath the barrel instantly distinguishes a Bren Gun from its Czechoslovakian prototypes, which have tubes extending virtually to the muzzle.

The earliest guns (Mark I or C. Mk I in Canada) had a complicated drum-type backsight graduated 200–1800yd, a folding handgrip beneath the butt and a folding shoulder strap on the butt heel. The top-mounted spring-and-gravity feed magazine is also most distinctive, owing to the marked forward curve required by the .303 cartridge, which has a tapering rimmed case. The barrel weighs about 2.85kg and can be detached simply by raising the latch and pulling the carrying handle forward.

Most Bren Guns will be encountered on bipods, though a few Brno-made tripods (copied from the Czechoslovakian ZB 206) acquired in 1937 were successful enough to allow an order for 3500 'Mounts, Tripod, Bren, Mark I' to be given to BSA Guns Ltd in 1939. Most of these were destined to spend their lives in store.

Bren Guns. **Top to bottom**: *a Mk I made in the Royal Australian Small Arms Factory, Lithgow, in 1942; a Mk IM, made by John Inglis & Company of Toronto in 1942; a Mk II, made by 'M 67' in 1943; and a short-barrelled Mk III.*

More than 400,000 Bren Guns were made in 1939–44, more than half emanating from the Enfield factory. Substantial quantities were made by Inglis of Toronto and more than 80,000 came from the Monotype Scheme, which allowed Bren Guns to be made by combining components made by an engineering syndicate which included the Daimler Co. Ltd and the Monotype Corporation Ltd. This explains the variety of manufacturers' marks that will be encountered.

Variants

Mark I (M) The Mk I (Modified) was introduced in the Autumn of 1940. This .303 Bren Gun had an angular (Mk I*) receiver, lacked the bracket for the optical sight and the barrel-handle base is a simple welded tube. The butt slide (Mk II) was simplified and a new bipod (Mk II) was fitted. The Mk I Modified Bren was made only by Enfield in Britain, though some were subsequently made in Australia in the Lithgow factory. These have Australian Mk 3 bipods. The C. Mk I Modified was essentially similar to the Enfield-made .303 equivalent.

Mark II Approved in June 1941 and made exclusively under the Monotype Scheme, this .303 pattern had a simpler body, a leaf-pattern backsight, a fixed cocking handle instead of the folding pattern, a simple stamped butt plate, a modified barrel with a detachable flash-hider/front-sight assembly, and a single recoil spring instead of two in the butt. The guns were originally made with Mk II bipods, but so many were repaired or altered at a later date that hybrids will be found. The Inglis-made Canadian C. Mk II Bren had a distinctive Canadian-made variant of the Mk 3 bipod.

Mark 2/1 Introduced in 1943, this was simply a .303 Mark II with a modified cocking handle and slide assembly, replacing the simplified fixed pattern developed in 1940.

Mark 3 Approved in May 1944, this .303 gun had a shorter 565mm barrel, a lightened receiver, simpler magazine-well and ejection-port covers and a plain (Mk 4) butt. Mk I or Mk 3 bipods were standard.

Mark 4 Approved concurrently with the Mk 3 to conserve supplies of raw material, this had a modified Mk II-type barrel cradle, noticeably less metal in the receiver and an ultra-short barrel with a new flash-hider.

Taken on 1 January 1945, British Official Photograph B.13280.XL shows a Bren gunner watching over a snowy No Man's Land in the British sector of the post-D-Day version of the Western Front.

Bren Gun, 7.62mm series

Britain

Light-support machine-gun
Made by the Royal Small Arms Factory, Enfield Lock, Middlesex, and by other contractors (*see* previous entry)
Specification L4A1
Calibre 7.62mm (.30)
Cartridge 7.62x51 NATO, rimless

Operation Gas operated, selective fire
Locking system Displacement of the bolt-tail into the receiver
Length 1133mm
Weight 10kg with bipod and empty magazine
Barrel 536mm, four grooves, right-hand twist
Feed Detachable thirty-round box magazine
Rate of fire 500±50rds/min
Muzzle velocity 825m/sec

A Royal Marine Bren gunner takes aim during winter exercises in Norway in 1976. Note the virtually straight-sided box magazine, which distinguishes the 7.62mm L4 conversions from the original .303 designs.

The British were well aware that the rimmed .303 cartridge was obsolescent, forming an Ideal Cartridge Panel in 1945, which predictably selected a .280 rimless round as the optimum, but the 'Cartridge, Ball, 7mm Mark 1Z' was abandoned in favour of the US 7.62 T65E3 cartridge-case in the 1950s.

Enfield had converted a few Bren Guns to .30-06 in 1947–8, for delivery to Italy, and guns in this chambering were also made in Canada (very few) and China (large numbers). Experiments were made with a .280 Bren Gun adaptation, modified from a Mk 3 and fitted with a magazine from the experimental EM-2 rifle.

As the Bren had a superlative war record, and as so many war-surplus guns were being held in store, the British authorities elected to convert the basic Mk 3 design to 7.62x51, making a pro- totype in 1954 from a wartime .303 Mk 3.

More than 1500 guns were issued from November 1957 as 'Guns, Machine, Light, 7.62mm L4A1'. They accepted an improved L3A2 magazine and were accompanied by two barrels weighing 2.72kg apiece.

Though the 7.62mm L4A4 proved most useful during the South Atlantic campaign in 1982, not least because it could accept standard twenty-round rifle magazines in an emergency, the basic design has been under threat of replacement by the 5.56mm LSW (q.v.),

even though many commentators regard the small-calibre weapon as a very poor performer compared with the tried and tested Bren Gun.

Variants

IA An Indian Army designation applied to conversions of Ishapur-made .303 Mk 3 Bren Guns to handle the 7.62x51mm NATO round. These are currently issued as 'Guns, Machine, Bren, 7.62mm IA'.

L4A1 Approved in 1957, this was a conversion of the .303 Mk 3 Bren Gun to handle NATO-standard 7.62mm ammunition. It accepted an improved L3A2 magazine and was accompanied by two barrels. Most L4A1 guns were subsequently converted to L4A2 standards.

L4A2 Converted from Mk 3 Brens in 1959–61, this accepted the finalised 7.62mm L4A1 magazine. The extractor and the ejector were improved, the breechblock was modified to make production easier, and changes were made to the magazine-well aperture.

L4A3 This was a variant of the 7.62mm L4A2, issued with a single chromed-bore barrel instead of two standard ones. Converted from the .303 Mk 3, only a few hundred were made for British service and all but 134 were sold to Libya in 1961–2.

L4A4 The standard British 7.62mm Bren Gun, accompanied by a single

chromium-lined spare barrel, about 12,000 of these were converted from wartime Mk II (rare) or Mk 3 (common) guns in 1960–1, or assembled from a mixture of newly made and old but unused parts.

L4A5 Converted from the .303 Mk II, this 7.62mm pattern was approved for Naval Service in April 1960. The guns are generally comparable with the L4A4, but were issued with two chromed-bore barrels.

L4A6 Approved in November 1960, this was a 7.62mm L4A1-type gun with the magazine-well aperture altered to accept the perfected L4A1 magazine instead of the L3A2. It also received a new chromed-bore barrel.

Besa Gun Britain

Tank machine-gun
Made by BSA Guns Ltd, Birmingham
Specification Besa Mk 3*
Calibre 7.92mm (.312)
Cartridge 7.92x57, rimless

Operation Gas operated, automatic fire only
Locking system Displacement of the bolt-tail into the receiver
Length 1105mm
Weight 21.65kg (gun only)

Barrel 740mm, four grooves, right-hand twist
Feed 225-round metal-link belt
Rate of fire 500±50rds/min
Muzzle velocity 825m/sec

Used for some time after the end of the Second World War, particularly in tanks and armoured vehicles, the 7.92mm Besa was derived from the Czechoslovakian vz. 37, shown here on the original Brno-designed tripod.

This was a straightforward derivative of the Czechoslovakian vz. 37 (ZB53) tank gun, derived from the vz. 30 light machine-gun, but with the construction altered to allow the barrel to recoil independently. This allowed the cartridge to be chambered at the completion of the backward stroke and fired as the parts were still running back to battery. This system minimised the effects of recoil, giving the Besa an enviable reputation for accuracy. The original 7.92mm chambering was retained, partly because of the urgency of the situation in 1938–9 but also to prevent the wholesale reconstruction that had delayed progress with the .303 Bren Gun.

The Mk I Besa was made only in small numbers as it was almost immediately replaced by the Mk II of 1940. This incorporated an adjustable accelerator giving two rates of fire, 'high' (750–850rds/min) for emergency local defence and 'low' (450–550rds/min) for normal use.

Additional marks introduced during the Second World War soon led to the simplified Mk 3 ('H' fire-rate only) and Mk 3* ('L' rate only). These have plain slab-sided fore-ends and unusually deep trigger guards. The Mark 3/2 and Mark 3/3 Besa machine-guns, introduced in 1952 and 1954 respectively, were apparently all refurbishments of Mk 3 and Mk 3* weapons made by BSA prior to 1946. They were restricted to the lower fire-rate. The 3/2 version had a modified feed cover and a new mounting block, while the 3/3 had an improved barrel with a larger gas vent and a modified gas cylinder to improve reliability with belts of mixed ammunition.

General-purpose ('Jimpy'), aircraft or vehicle machine-gun
Made by the Royal Small Arms Factory, Enfield Lock, and by Royal Ordnance plc, Enfield Lock and Nottingham
Specification L7A1
Data for light-support version
Calibre 7.62mm (.30)
Cartridge 7.62x51 NATO, rimless
Operation Gas operated, automatic fire only
Locking system Displacement of the bolt into the receiver
Length 1232mm
Weight 10.9kg (with bipod)
Barrel 597mm (excluding flash-hider), four grooves, right-hand twist
Feed Metal-link belt
Rate of fire 875±125rds/min
Muzzle velocity 840m/sec

Trials undertaken in Britain in 1956 – with the X11E2, the US M60, Belgium's FN MAG, a French AAT Mle 52, Danish Madsen-Saetters, and the Swiss SIG MG 55 – proved that the MAG was the best all-round weapon. The MAG was adopted in 1958, the first Enfield-made guns being distributed in the summer of 1963.

The gas-operated 'Gun, Machine, General Purpose, 7.62mm L7A1' has a sturdy tilting-bolt lock. It is usually encountered with a bipod and a pistol grip, and feeds a 250-round disintegrating-link belt from the left side. Fitted with the standard wood butt, for use as a light machine-gun, the L7A1 may be issued with the 13.65kg 'Mounting, Tripod, Machine Gun, L4A1' and 'Sight, Unit, Infantry, Trilux C2' (SUIT) can transform the L7 into a medium-support

The British L7 GPMG, without its butt, mounted on the standard tripod. Note the C2A1 optical sight to facilitate long-range fire.

weapon. The standard barrel weighs 2.73kg, but a blank-firing L3A1 attachment can be fitted when required.

Variants

L7A2 Introduced in 1963, this differs from the L7A1 by the addition of a second feed pawl in the feed mechanism and mounts for a special fifty-round belt-bag on the left side of the receiver, enabling it to serve as a light machine-gun.

L8A1 and L8A2 Dating originally from 1978, fitted in the Chieftain (L8A1) and Challenger (L8A2) tanks, these have bore-evacuators and variable-aperture gas regulators. They can also accept solenoid trigger systems.

L19A1 Not issued for general service, this heavy-barrel L7A1 has been made in small numbers for specialist support roles in which sustained fire is required. The weight of the barrel reduces the effects of heating and extends the periods between barrel changes.

L20A1 Destined for helicopter use, this is a combination of the L8 body, with its distinctive gas regulator, and an L7 barrel lacking the evacuator needed for vehicle use. The L20A1 can be adapted to accept ammunition belts from either side of the feed block.

L37A1 and L37A2 These tank/vehicle guns are little more than L8s with new L6A1 barrels. Unlike the L8, however,

L37 guns are designed to be dismounted: an L1A2 barrel, a bipod, a butt and a pistol-grip assembly are usually carried aboard vehicles to permit emergency ground use.

L43A1 A ranging coaxial vehicle/local-defence gun, this has a special additional barrel bearing between the gas block and the muzzle.

L41A1, L45A1 and L46A1 These are all non-firing instructional versions cannibalised from L8A1 tank, L37A1 tank and L7A2 ground guns respectively.

Taken in Omagh in June 1986, this shows two men of the 3rd Light Infantry Brigade. One man (right) carries an L4 Bren Gun, without its magazine, while his colleague displays an L7 GPMG.

48

L86 LSW

Light Support Weapon
Made by Royal Ordnance plc,
Nottingham
Specification XL86E1
Data from Royal Ordnance promotional
literature, 1986
Calibre 5.56mm (.223)

Cartridge 5.56x45, rimless
Operation Gas operated, selective fire
Locking system Rotating bolt,
engaging the receiver
Length 900mm
Weight 6.88kg (with bipod and loaded
magazine)

Barrel 646mm, six grooves, right-hand
twist
Feed Thirty-round detachable box
magazine
Rate of fire 775±75rds/min
Muzzle velocity 970m/sec

The current version of the British 5.56mm L86A1 LSW, showing the straight-bottom receiver and extended bipod-mounting rail which distinguish production guns from the prototypes. The LSW lacks a detachable barrel and, consequently, cannot sustain fire in the manner of the L4 Bren Gun.

The LSW has replaced the old but popular Bren Gun, as well as the L7A2 GPMG in its light machine-gun role, and has been touted commercially as the 'Enfield Engager'. The project originated in the 4.85mm XL65E4, but NATO rejected the 4.85mm round in favour of 5.56mm and the XL65 was replaced by the XL73E2.

The Ministry of Defence announced that the 5.56mm XL73 was 'ready for service' in the mid-1970s, but severe accuracy and reliability problems delayed its approval for a decade. The LSW was originally designed to keep 80 per cent parts commonality with the L85 (SA-80) rifle, but experience quickly suggested that this goal was unrealistic. Consequently, the two designs have diverged in several important respects and the current L86A1 (XL86E1 prior to 1987) carries its bipod on an extension of the frame.

The issue of the 4x 'Sight, Unit, Small Arms, Trilux' (SUSAT) as a standard fixture gives the L86 some important advantages over the Bren Gun, but the absence of an exchangeable barrel – even though the LSW fires automatically from an open-bolt position – restricts support-fire capabilities. The magazine position is poor, almost always disturbing aim during reloading and the high profile, accentuated by the straight-line configuration and the SUSAT sight, exposes the firer to danger if sufficient cover is unavailable.

Type 67 and others

General-purpose machine-gun
Made by China North Industries
Corporation (Norinco)
Specification Type 67
Data from a Chinese manual, *c.*1972
Calibre 7.62mm (.30)
Cartridge 7.62x54 Type 53, rimmed

Operation Gas operated, automatic fire
only
Locking system Flaps on the bolt
engaging the receiver walls
Length 1345mm
Weight 11.7kg (plus 13.5kg for the
tripod)

Barrel 805mm (including flash-hider),
four grooves, right-hand twist
Feed Fifty-round belt drum or 250-
round belt box
Rate of fire 650±50rds/min
Muzzle velocity 865m/sec

Though the Type 67 is widely used by Chinese militia units, the Type 80 – a copy of the Soviet PK as shown here – is more common in the armed forces.

The Chinese have copied Soviet-style machine-guns, making them in huge quantities. However, the guns are usually difficult to distinguish from their prototypes, excepting in detail and by their markings. Details of the 7.62mm Type 53 light machine-gun (DPM), 7.62mm Type 53 heavy machine-gun (SG) 12.7mm Type 54 (Norinco Model 17, DShKM), 7.62mm Types 56 and 56-1 (RPD), 14.5mm Type 56 (KPV), 7.62mm Type 57 (Norinco Model 18, SGM), 7.62mm Type 58 (RP-46), 12.7mm Type 59 (modified DShKM), 7.62mm Type 59T (SGMT) will all be found in the Soviet section. The Types 74 and 81, based on the RPK and the Chinese Type 68 militia rifle respectively, are considered to be heavy automatic rifles instead of machine-guns. Guns of these patterns have all been exported extensively and were regularly encountered by US personnel fighting in Vietnam.

The Type 67 light machine-gun is an indigenous design, though features have been taken from a number of other guns. The feed system is an adaptation of the pre-war Chinese Type 24 Maxim; the tipping-block locking mechanism and the piston system have been adapted from the Czechoslovakian ZB vz. 26; the trigger is basically that of the DPM; the design of the gas regulator has been adapted from the RPD; and the barrel change is the perfected SGM type. The

result is a sturdy and serviceable machine-gun, if somewhat heavy.

The charging handle on the right side of the receiver must be lifted before the action can be retracted and the safety catch, on the right side of the receiver above the trigger, must be set to the fire position before this is attempted – otherwise the mechanism will jam. Unlike most of Soviet belt-feed 7.62mm guns, the Type 67 handles a belt made of open links joined by spring-wire spirals. These allow the clumsy rimmed 7.62x54 rounds to be pushed straight through the links, whereas guns such as the PK have to pull the cartridges backward before they can be rammed forward into the chamber. The Type 67 feeds from the right, with the open side of the link downward. The backsight is a pivoting leaf, with windage and elevation drums on the sight block. A small pillar on top of the leaf can be used with a ring-type anti-aircraft sight which slots into dovetails in the top surface of the receiver.

The barrel can be changed by lifting the feed cover on top of the receiver, removing the belt, pressing the barrel-retaining catch, then pulling the barrel forward and away from the breech. A carrying handle attached to the barrel makes this process easier. A new barrel is pushed into position and the retaining catch returned to the locked position. An

SGM-type headspace adjuster is provided, and the regulator has three positions to adapt to variations in operating conditions or ammunition pressure. The Chinese tripod, with one leg at the front and two at the rear, offers a traverse of 80 degrees, a maximum elevation of about 10 degrees and a depression of about 30 degrees.

Variants
Type 67-1 This has a lightweight tripod with an improved gun-attachment system, the weight of the mount being merely 5.6kg. The gun retains the full-length barrel, giving it an overall length of 1345mm and a weight of about 11.5kg.
Type 67-2 Derived from the 67-1, this has a shorter barrel than its predecessor. Overall length is 1250mm, weight being about 10kg.
Type 67-2C The differences between this gun and the 67-2 are not yet clearly understood, but may refer to an alteration in the sights – perhaps the fitting of a base for thermal imaging or electro-optical patterns.

Heavy anti-aircraft machine-gun
Made by China North Industries
Corporation (Norinco)
Specification Type 77
Calibre 12.7mm (.50)
Cartridge 12.7x108 Type 54, rimless
Operation Gas operated, automatic fire
only
Locking system Flaps on the bolt
engaging the receiver wall
Length 2150mm
Weight 56.1kg (without mount)
Barrel 1575mm (approx), eight grooves,
right-hand twist
Feed Sixty-round metal-link belt
Rate of fire 700±50rds/min
Muzzle velocity 800m/sec

Based on the Degtyarev flap-lock guns –
the Soviet DShKM (q.v.) has been made
in quantity in China – the Type 77 has a
very distinctive tubular receiver. A Type
85 vehicle gun embodies the same
action, but is shorter and lighter than the
standard pattern; it may be mounted
coaxially with the main armament of a
tank or armoured car, often in conjunction with a solenoid trigger and a
cable-type charging system. These guns
lack fixed sights.

The Chinese 12.7mm Type 77 machine-gun.

Light machine-gun
Made by Československá Zbrojovka, Brno
Specification ZB vz. 30, standard
pattern
Calibre 7.9mm (.311)
Cartridge 7.92x57, rimless
Operation Gas operated, selective fire
Locking system Displacement of the
bolt-tail into the receiver
Length 1160mm
Weight 9.6kg with bipod
Barrel 675mm, four grooves, right-
hand twist
Feed Detachable thirty-round box
magazine
Rate of fire 600±50rds/min

Muzzle velocity 765m/sec (heavy-
bullet ammunition)

This gun originated in a series of guns
designed in the early 1920s by Vaclav
Holek for Zbrojovka Praga. Beginning with
the Praga 1, Holek developed the Praga
2a and I-23 before producing the
perfected M-24 'Hand-held Machine
Gun'. Minor changes were made to
facilitate mass production, and the M-24
became the ZB vz. 26.

Series production began immediately
in Brno for the armed forces, but
improvements in the bolt and gas system
soon led to the vz. 27. The principal

difference concerned the method of
unlocking the bolt, which was achieved by
cam tracks on the outside surface of the
piston-rod extension (vz. 26), acting on the
front of the breechblock, or by a cam
surface on the piston post (vz. 27) acting
towards the rear of the breechblock.

The vz. 27 was not standardised by the
Czechoslovakian Army, where it was
superseded by the vz. 30. This had an
additional safety lug on the barrel locknut
collar, a stronger piston and a better gas-
regulation system. Guns of this type were
made under licence in China, Spain and
Persia (Iran), and may be marked
accordingly.

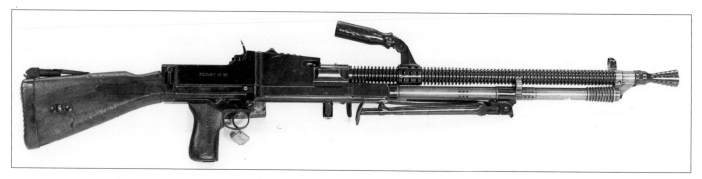

The 7.9mm Czechoslovakian ZB vz. 26. Except for the finned barrel and extended gas tube, the gun bears a considerable
resemblance to its lineal descendant, the .303 British Bren Gun.

Light-support machine-gun
Made by Československá Zbrojovka, Brno
Specification vz. 52/57
Calibre 7.62mm (.30)
Cartridge 7.62x39 M43, rimless
Operation Gas operated, selective fire
Locking system Tipping breech-bolt
Length 1041mm
Weight 7.95kg with bipod
Barrel 685mm, four grooves, right-hand twist
Feed 100-round belt or detachable box magazine with twenty-five rounds
Rate of fire 900rds/min (box), 1150rds/min (belt)
Muzzle velocity 745m/sec

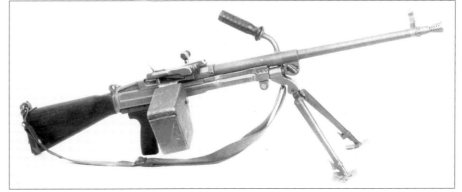

Based on the ZB vz. 30 described previously, the vz. 52 light machine-gun embodies a convertible belt/box feed. It was originally chambered for the special Czechoslovakian 7.62x45 rimless cartridge.

The gun fires from an open bolt, but is charged in an unusual way. Pressing a latch on the left side of the receiver above the pistol grip releases the trigger/grip group from its locked position. Pressing the trigger allows the entire assembly to be slid forward until releasing the trigger allows the sear to

Two views of a 7.62mm Czechoslovakian vz. 52/57 light machine-gun captured in Angola by the South African Defence Forces. The method of pressing the trigger controls the mode of fire, without requiring an additional selector.

engage with the piston. Pulling the assembly back to its original position retracts the piston and bolt carrier, the trigger/grip unit locks back into its original position and the gun is ready to be fired. Locking is effected when the cam ramps on the bolt carrier force lugs on the tail of the breech-bolt upward into recesses in the side walls of the receiver. The safety catch lies on the left rear of the receiver; when applied, it locks the sear and prevents the trigger group being moved to charge the gun.

The two-position regulators can be altered by using the combination tool supplied with each gun. Barrels can be removed by releasing the latch and opening the feed cover. The cover can then be rotated laterally, to the right (looking from the rear), so that the interrupted threads on the barrel and barrel nut are disengaged. This allows the barrel to be withdrawn forwards. Unfortunately, the bipod, attached to the barrel, has to be removed from the old barrel and reattached to the new one before the parts can be reassembled.

The mode of fire can be controlled simply by changing the point of pressure on the trigger, which had two curves – uppermost for automatic operation, lowermost for single shots. The machined receiver is inserted in a stamped body, seeking to simplify production and simultaneously reduce weight.

The vz. 52 was made in some numbers and, apart from comparatively limited belt-lifting abilities, was as efficient as most of the guns in its class introduced in the decade immediately after the end of the Second World War. However, no sooner had series production begun than the Soviet authorities brought pressure to bear on the Czechoslovakians; in the interests of Warsaw Pact standardisation, therefore, the vz. 52 was redesigned to chamber the Soviet 7.62x39 M43 cartridge and reintroduced as the vz. 52/57. The new cartridge was substantially less powerful than the vz. 52 pattern and there is some evidence to show that the machine-gun did not work as efficiently after the change had been made. This has often happened in cases where weapons have been designed to work with ammunition offering particular pressure/time characteristics and are then altered to fire something else.

Vz. 59 Czechoslovakia

General-purpose machine-gun
Made by Československá Zbrojovka, Brno
Specification vz. 59
Data for standard heavy-barrel version
Calibre 7.62mm (.30)
Cartridge 7.62x54, rimmed

Operation Gas operated, automatic fire only
Locking system Displacement of the bolt into the receiver
Length 1216mm
Weight 9.31kg (without mount)

Barrel 693mm, four grooves, right-hand twist
Feed Metal-link belt
Rate of fire 750±50rds/min
Muzzle velocity 830m/sec (light-bullet ammunition)

The Czechoslovakian vz. 59N on its bipod. The carrying handle has been rotated sideways as a prelude to detaching the barrel. **57**

This was a derivative of the vz. 52/57 described previously, embodying the same tipping-bolt system, but adapted to fulfil differing roles. Unlike most Soviet designs, the vz. 59 handles open-pocket belts, which enable the cumbersome rimmed cartridges to be pushed directly into the chamber instead of needing to be drawn back and then moved downward during the opening stroke of the bolt (cf., Soviet SGM and PK).

Two-position regulators were standard and the vz. 59 was charged in the same way as the vz. 52/57, and shared a similar barrel-locking system. The standard heavy barrel weighs 3.8kg, about 600g more than the lightweight alternative. The basic fifty-round belt weighs 1.38kg when loaded, the fifty-round and 250-round containers adding 600g and 2.22kg respectively. The belts can be joined, so that a full 250-round container weighs about 6.9kg.

The original guns had a backsight with a pivoting leaf in the form of an inverted horseshoe, drums on the sight block controlling windage and elevation; later versions, however, have a conventional squared leaf with elevation controlled by spring catches. The sights lie on the top rear of the receiver behind the feed cover. The cover must be lifted vertically before the vz. 59 can be attached to its tripod, as the rear of the gun has to be passed beneath the traversing arc before the lugs on top of the receiver can be pinned to lugs on the mount. Many guns will be found with a 4x optical sight weighing about 380g, which can be clamped either to the receiver or the tripod body. The sight has an illuminated reticle and can be adjusted for windage and elevation.

The tripod weighs 9.95kg and can be adapted for anti-aircraft fire with the assistance of extension tubes. Barrel-axis height can be adjusted to 300-500mm above the ground, maximum elevation being about 21.5 degrees; traverse between the limit-stops is restricted to about 43 degrees, but 360-degree manual traverse is possible if the stops are removed.

Variants
Vz. 59L This light-barrelled gun, mounted on a bipod, is the standard light-support version of the basic design. The gun is 1116mm overall with a 593mm barrel and weighs 8.67kg with its bipod.

Vz. 59N A derivative of the basic design chambering the rimless 7.62x51 NATO cartridge, this was offered for export in the 1960s. Purchases seem to have been few and far between. Guns of this type have a four-position gas regulator controlled by the carrying handle. The handle-latch is pressed to permit the handle to rotate until a pointer on the handle aligns with the relevant notch in the gas cylinder, allowing the regulator to be rotated to the appropriate setting. Positions marked '1', '2' and '3' are used to adjust to differing conditions or ammunition, whereas '4' gives high-speed fire (1000–1100rds/min) suited to anti-aircraft use.

Vz. 59T This tank and armoured-vehicle gun was usually mounted coaxially with the main armament. It was customarily fitted with a solenoid-type firing mechanism and a cable-type retractor instead of a conventional charging handle.

Madsen-Saetter

Denmark

General-purpose machine-gun;
Maskingevaer Madsen-Saetter
Made by Dansk Industri Syndikat,
Kompagni Madsen A/S, Copenhagen

Specification Madsen-Saetter SFMG
Mark 4
Data from Dansk Industri Syndikat
handbook

Calibre 7.62mm (.30)
Cartridge 7.62x51 NATO, rimless
Operation Gas operated, automatic fire
only

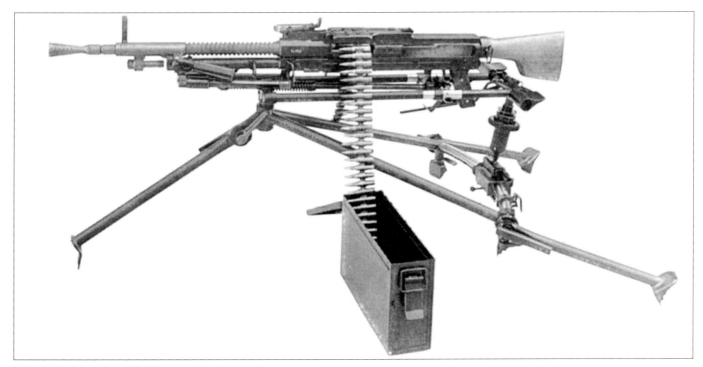

The Danish Madsen-Saetter on its buffered tripod mount.

Locking system Flaps in the bolt carrier engage the receiver walls
Length 1165mm
Weight 10.8kg (with bipod and light barrel)
Barrel 480mm without flash-hider, four grooves, right-hand twist
Feed Metal-link belt with forty-nine rounds
Rate of fire 650–1000rds/min depending on configuration
Muzzle velocity 835m/sec with SS77 ball cartridges

This represented one of DISA's last forays into the small-arms market. The Madsen-Saetter was a conventional belt-feed design, with a gas-piston tube beneath the barrel and a bolt which was locked in place by flaps on the bolt-carrier block engaging the receiver walls. Like most machine-guns of its class, it fired from the open bolt position to minimise the chances of a cook-off. The charging handle lay on the right side of the receiver, with a push-through safety catch in front of the trigger. The Madsen-Saetter could be field stripped in a matter of seconds, without the assistance of tools.

The gun had a finned quick-detachable barrel carrying the blade-type front sight, the tangent-leaf backsight (graduated 200–1400m) appearing on the receiver-top in front of the feed tray. A long-range rotary (dial) sight could be provided to order. Most guns were fitted with a bipod, even if tripod-mounted for sustained-fire roles, and had wooden 'straight-through' in-line butts.

The Madsen-Saetter was offered in a variety of chamberings, from 6.5mm to .30-06 and 7.92mm, but was only made in small numbers. The standard light machine-gun was supplied on a bipod, with a barrel weighing about 2.45kg. Alternatively, the Madsen-Saetter could be configured in a sustained-fire (SF) role with a heavy barrel weighing about 2.9kg and a tripod mount. The bores and chambers were customarily chromium-plated to extend their useful lives.

Each feed belt of forty-nine rounds could be joined to another with an additional cartridge, though the light machine-guns were customarily issued with an ammunition box holding a single belt. The standard tripod had a buffered gun cradle. It weighed about 11.7kg and could give an above ground bore-height of 355–620mm; traverse was limited to about 17 degrees either side of the centreline and maximum elevation was only about 12 degrees. However, by altering the position of the legs, firing could be undertaken at depressions of up to about 40 degrees and elevations as great as 28 degrees. Accessories included a blank-firing booster, spare barrels and cleaning equipment.

AAT52

*General-purpose, aircraft or vehicle
machine-gun; Arme Automatique
Transformable, Modèle 52*
Made in factories in Saint-Étienne and
Châtellerault (now part of GIAT)

Specification AAT52, *Version
Mitrailleuse* or heavy barrel version
Calibre 7.5mm (.295)
Cartridge 7.5x54 Mle 29, rimless
Operation Delayed blowback,

automatic fire only
Locking system None (*see* text)
Length 1245mm (butt extended),
1080mm (butt folded)
Weight 11.37kg (21.97kg with tripod)

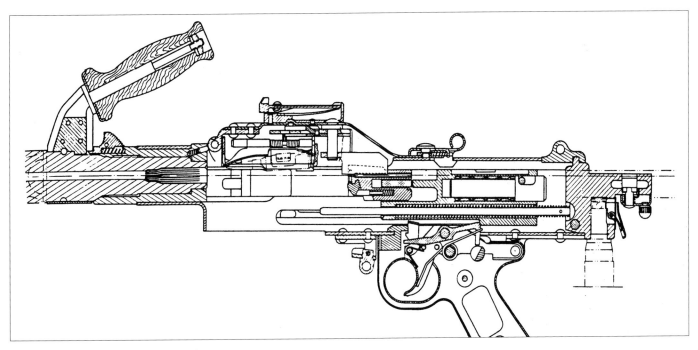

A longitudinal section of the AAT action.

Barrel 600mm, four grooves, right-hand twist
Feed Metal-link belt
Rate of fire 700±50rds/min
Muzzle velocity 840m/sec

The standard French GPMG since the 1950s, the original 7.5mm AAT has often been reckoned as unsatisfactory outside the confines of France and some of the former French colonies, largely owing to the lack of a positive breech lock. However, the successful adaptation of the gun to handle the 7.62x51 NATO cartridge has given it a new lease of life.

The AAT fires from an open-bolt position, feeding from left to right. The breech is held closed at the moment of firing by a lever-like 'retarder', which pivots against a shoulder in the receiver to push the heavier rear portion of the two-piece bolt backward. This is just sufficient to slow the initial movement of the front part of the block until the chamber pressure has dropped far enough to allow extraction to begin. A fluted chamber prevents the spent case sticking to the chamber walls.

The AAT fires a disintegrating-link belt with a pitch of 14.7mm, which can be adapted to hold 7.5mm or 7.62mm cartridges, depending on the calibre of the gun, and can also be used with guns such as the Heckler & Koch HK21 series (q.v.). An empty fifty-round belt weighs

137g, rising to 1335g loaded (7.62mm version). External appearance is most distinctive, with a unique tubular construction. Occasionally encountered on tripod mounts, the US M2 pattern being favoured, the AAT will also be found with a bipod at the muzzle and an adjustable monopod beneath the receiver behind the pistol grip.

Though the French still hold substantial quantities of the Fusil Mitrailleur Mle 24/29 and Mitrailleuse Mle 31 (MAC31) in reserve, this is simply because the AAT has never been made in large enough quantities. Individual AAT guns are still being used by NATO ammunition makers to test 7.62mm cartridges for acceptability.

Variants

AAT52, Version Fusil Mitrailleur Also known as the AAT Légère, this offers a lightweight 50cm barrel, a bipod, and a retractable monopod beneath the folding butt. This version is about 100mm shorter than the sustained-fire pattern and weighs only 9.97kg. Muzzle velocity is about 825m/sec.

AAT52 de 7.62 N-F1 This is a modernised form of the original AAT, chambered for the 7.62x51 NATO cartridge. It is available in two versions: as a bipod-mounted light-support weapon (Type fusil-mitrailleur) or on a tripod (Type mitrailleuse).

AAT52 de 7.62 N-F1 Char No. 1 The fixed or coaxial tank and vehicle gun in the series, this has been made in two subvarieties – Type A and Type B, the later being specially waterproofed. Tank/vehicle guns are usually heavy barrelled and may have solenoid firing systems.

AAT52 de 7.62 N-F1 Char No.2 The flexibly mounted tank/vehicle version has a light barrel, a manual trigger and sometimes a shoulder stock.

AAT52 de 7.62 N-F1 Avion No.1 – No.4 Intended for use in fixed-wing aircraft and helicopters, these guns may be encountered with a variety of fittings, including solenoid triggers. Apart from No. 4, which has a manual trigger and sights, they are usually installed in rigid mounts.

General-purpose machine-gun;
Maschinengewehr Modell 3
Made by Rheinmetall GmbH, Düsseldorf
Specification MG 3
Calibre 7.62mm (.30)
Cartridge 7.62x51 NATO, rimless
Operation Recoil operated, automatic
fire only
Locking system Rollers on the bolt
head engage slots cut in the barrel
extension
Length 1225mm
Weight 10.5kg (plus 1kg for bipod)
Barrel 530mm excluding lock-piece,
four grooves, right-hand twist
Feed Metal-link belt
Rate of fire 700±50rds/min (with 550
light bolt)
Muzzle velocity 820m/sec

The MG 42 was introduced during the
Second World War to replace the MG 34,
which, though beautifully made, had
proved to be too susceptible to jamming
in muddy or dusty conditions. The
essence of the MG 42 was its roller-
locked breech, operated by allowing the
barrel to recoil far enough to let the
rollers disengage the cage-like lock-
piece extension on the barrel. The bolt
then ran back against the resistance

*The German MG 3, made by Rheinmetall, is a lineal successor to the legendary wartime
MG 42. Shown here are **top** an MG 3 on its standard German tripod and **above** an
Austrian MG 58 on a Steyr-Daimler-Puch tripod.*

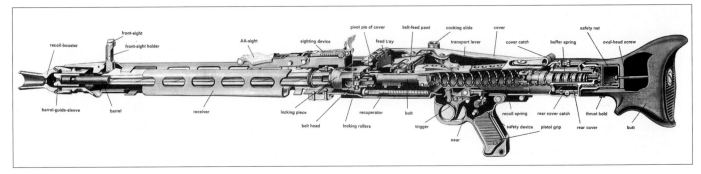

A cutaway drawing of the MG 3, showing the principal parts.

offered by a return spring.

The MG 42 was surprisingly crudely made by German standards, but rapidly attained a fearsome reputation. This was partly due to its unusually high rate of fire – the noise of firing was generally reckoned to resemble ripping linoleum, and gained it the sobriquet *Hitlersäge*, Hitler's saw. However, it was evidently prone to jamming and not as accurate as some rival designs.

After the war ended, research continued in Spain until the CETME rifle was perfected. When production of firearms was permitted in the Federal Republic of Germany, it was only natural that the MG 42 should be revived. Beginning with the MG 42/59 (*Bundeswehr* designation MG 1), revised by Rheinmetall to chamber the 7.62mm short-case NATO cartridge instead of the

original 7.9x57mm version, the design had evolved by 1968 into the MG 3.

However, apart from the addition of an anti-aircraft sight, the Rheinmetall MG 3 and the original MG 42 remain essentially similar. An additional retaining pawl holds the belt up to the gun when the feed cover is raised, but the barrel can still be changed simply by releasing the locking latch and swinging it out of the slot in the right side of the barrel casing. The backsight is a tangent-leaf graduated 200–1200m, with additional distances to 2200m available when the leaf is raised vertically. An anti-aircraft sight is also fitted as standard beneath a hinged cover.

The cyclic rate can be altered by changing the bolt, the rear cover and the booster attached to the front of the barrel casing, where it helps to support the

muzzle. The heavy bolt marked '950' weighs 950g, whereas the light bolt, marked '550', weighs merely 550g; used with 'R' and 'N' top-covers, cyclic rates are respectively about 700rds/min and 1300rds/min. The oscillating feed arm is operated by a large stud on top of the rear of the bolt body.

Most guns were used with hanging belts, which tend to promote jamming, until Heckler & Koch introduced a special fifty-round drum in the 1980s. Made largely of plastics and designed to operate within temperatures ranging from -35°C to +63°C, this weighed 307g empty and 1755g loaded; it is 187mm high (carrying handle uppermost), 137mm wide and about 100m thick. A transparent strip set into the rear surface of the drum allows the firer to assess the availability of ammunition at a glance.

The charging handle protrudes from the right side of the receiver and the entire top plate can be lifted to give access to the feed tray. The MG 3 will operate with DM1 fixed-link or DM6 and M13 disintegrating-link belts interchangeably. The DM1, with links wire-laced together, has a pitch of 17.2mm; a fifty-round belt weighs about 150g empty or 1348g loaded, plus about 20g for the tab attached to the first section of belt to facilitate feeding. The disintegrating DM6 pattern, with a pitch of 15.1mm, weighs 212g empty and 1410g loaded (fifty rounds), with an additional 15g feed tab. The relevant figures for the US M13, with a pitch of 14.7mm, are 21g empty, 1408g loaded and an additional 13g for the feed tab. The M13 links have a large circular hole in the body, distinguishing them from the plain DM6 pattern.

Variants

MG 1 This designation was applied to the MG 42/59 (*see* below) after it had been adopted as the standard weapon of the *Bundeswehr*.

MG 1A1 An improved form of the MG 1, these guns had chromium-plated bores and chambers and could only fire fixed-link DM1 belts.

MG 1A2 A minor variant of the MG 1A1, these guns could fire continuous DM1 or disintegrating-link M13 belts interchangeably.

MG 1A3 This was simply a minor adaptation of the MG 1A1, restricted to fixed-link belts but with an improved muzzle booster.

MG 2 These were pre-1945 examples of the MG 42 converted to chamber the 7.62x51 NATO cartridge.

MG 42/59 Made by Rheinmetall, this was the first designation applied to newly made derivatives of the wartime MG 42 chambered for the 7.62mm NATO cartridge.

Licensed versions The MG 42/59 and its derivatives have been made in several countries. The Austrian Army has used converted ex-German MG 42s and new Rheinmetall-made MG 42/59 guns as the 'MG 58', alongside essentially similar MG 74 guns made under licence by Steyr-Daimler-Puch AG. Italian MG 42/59 guns are the products of Pietro Beretta of Gardone Val Trompia (maker of bolts and other components), Luigi Franci SpA of Fornaci (barrels, trigger assemblies), and Whitehead Moto-Fides SA of Livorno (receiver bodies). They are known as *Fucile Mitragliatore* or *Mitragliatrice*, mounted on bipods and tripods respectively. Guns have been made in Spain and in Portugal. Turkish MG 3s are the products of Silahsan Hafif Silah Sanayi ve Tikaret AS of Kirikkale, a division of Makina ve Kimya Endüstrisi Kurumu (MKE). Modified versions have been made by Zavodi Crvena Zastava (ZCZ) in Yugoslavia and by SIG in Switzerland. Guns of this general type have been used in countries ranging from Austria to the Sudan.

The MG 42/MG 3 series has been made under licence in several countries. This picture shows a Turkish-made pattern.

Heckler & Koch HK11 series   Germany

Light-support machine-gun; HK-Maschinengewehr Modell 11
Made by Heckler & Koch GmbH, Oberndorf am Neckar
Specification HK11 light machine-gun
Data from a brochure dated October 1971
Calibre 7.62mm (.30)
Cartridge 7.62x51 NATO, rimless

Operation Delayed blowback, selective fire
Locking system Rollers delay the opening of the breech
Length 1020mm
Weight 6.2kg without bipod or magazine (bipod adds 0.6kg)
Barrel 450mm without flash-hider, polygonal rifling, right-hand twist

Feed Twenty-round detachable box magazine or eighty-round 'dual drum'
Rate of fire 850±50rds/min
Muzzle velocity 780m/sec

Note: later literature gives an overall length of 1030mm, a weight of 7.7kg with bipod, and a cyclic rate averaging 800rds/min

66 *The original version of the HK11, with the 'lettered' selector positions. Note the short barrel casing and the drum-like magazine.*

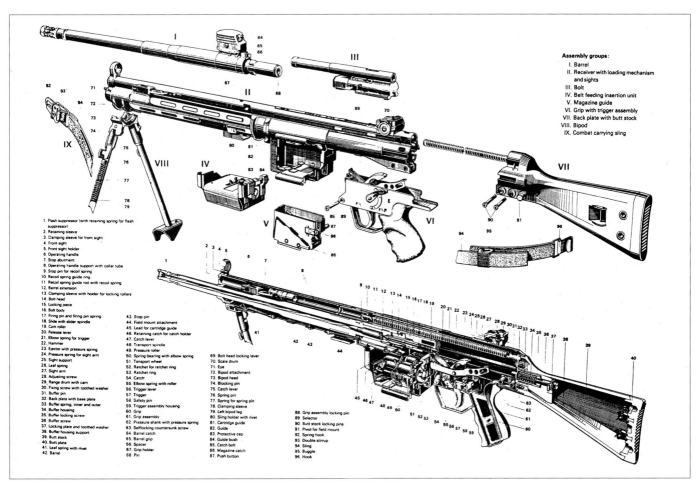

Assembly groups:

I. Barrel
II. Receiver with loading mechanism and sights
III. Bolt
IV. Belt feeding insertion unit
V. Magazine guide
VI. Grip with trigger assembly
VII. Back plate with butt stock
VIII. Bipod
IX. Combat carrying sling

1. Flash suppressor (with retaining spring for flash suppressor)
2. Retaining sleeve
3. Clamping sleeve for front sight
4. Front sight
5. Front sight holder
6. Operating handle
7. Stop abutment
8. Operating handle support with collar tube
9. Stop pin for recoil spring
10. Recoil spring guide ring
11. Recoil spring guide rod with recoil spring
12. Barrel extension
13. Clamping sleeve with holder for locking rollers
14. Bolt head
15. Locking piece
16. Bolt body
17. Firing pin and firing pin spring
18. Slide with slider spindle
19. Cam roller
20. Release lever
21. Elbow spring for trigger
22. Hammer
23. Ejector with pressure spring
24. Pressure spring for sight arm
25. Sight support
26. Leaf spring
27. Sight arm
28. Adjusting screw
29. Range drum with cam
30. Fixing screw with toothed washer
31. Buffer pin
32. Back plate with base plate
33. Buffer spring, inner and outer
34. Buffer housing
35. Buffer locking screw
36. Buffer sleeve
37. Locking plate and toothed washer
38. Buffer housing support
39. Butt stock
40. Butt plate
41. Leaf spring with rivet
42. Barrel

43. Stop pin
44. Field mount attachment
45. Lead for cartridge guide
46. Retaining catch for catch holder
47. Catch lever
48. Transport spindle
49. Pressure roller
50. Spring bearing with elbow spring
51. Transport wheel
52. Ratchet for ratchet ring
53. Ratchet ring
54. Catch
55. Elbow spring with roller
56. Trigger lever
57. Trigger
58. Safety pin
59. Trigger assembly housing
60. Grip
61. Grip assembly
62. Pressure shank with pressure spring
63. Selflocking countersunk screw
64. Barrel catch
65. Barrel grip
66. Spacer
67. Grip holder
68. Pin

69. Bolt head locking lever
70. Scale drum
71. Eye
72. Bipod attachment
73. Bipod head
74. Blocking pin
75. Catch lever
76. Spring pin
77. Spring for spring pin
78. Clamping sleeve
79. Left bipod leg
80. Sling holder with rivet
81. Cartridge guide
82. Guide
83. Protective cap
84. Guide bush
85. Catch bolt
86. Magazine catch
87. Push button

88. Grip assembly locking pin
89. Selector
90. Butt stock locking pins
91. Pivot for field mount
92. Spring hook
93. Double stirrup
94. Sling
95. Buggle
96. Hook

An exploded-view drawing of a typical HK11.

67

The HK11A1 was an improved form of the HK11. Note the design of the butt, facilitating a left-hand hold, the cutaway casing allowing the barrel to be withdrawn, and the repetition of the selector markings alongside the end of the selector-lever spindle.

The origins of these guns lay with the recoil-operated MG 42 (q.v.), but even before the Second World War ended, the MG 42 had been adapted into a delayed-blowback version tested experimentally as the MG 45. The German military authorities were profoundly suspicious of anything that lacked a breech-lock. Experiments with the MG 45 and an essentially similar assault rifle, the StG 45 (M), were still continuing when hostilities ceased. Work recommenced in Spain in the late 1940s, with the assistance of expatriate Mauser engineers, and eventually resulted in the CETME rifle.

When the Germans were permitted to rearm in the late 1950s, the *Bundeswehr*, reluctant to accept the FN FAL, settled upon the CETME. The Spanish gun had been submitted by Heckler & Koch, then best known as a machine-tool maker, but a production licence was negotiated and the first true G3 rifles were made in 1960.

Work was initially split between Rheinmetall and Heckler & Koch to speed re-equipment, but, after the initial contract had been completed, Heckler &

Koch continued work alone. Soon, the basic roller-lock action had been incorporated in a wide range of handguns, rifles and machine-guns.

By 1988, the success of the design was such that Heckler & Koch firearms were being made under licence in fourteen countries.

The HK11, the first of the company's machine-guns to be introduced, is basically a G3 rifle. When the gun fires, the breechblock immediately tries to move backward, though the opening of the breech is delayed by a combination of the frictional resistance of the rollers against the receiver walls, the inertia required to push the rear part of the bolt backward to allow the rollers to retract, and the pressure of the return spring opposing the opening of the breech. Once the rollers have been moved far enough inward, the bolt runs back to eject a spent case; the return spring then returns the parts to their original position, stripping a new round into the chamber, and the rollers move back out into their recesses. The gun can then be fired again, a mechanical safety feature ensuring that this cannot happen until the breech is properly closed.

One disadvantage of this system is that the breech begins to open before the residual pressure inside the spent case has dropped sufficiently, leading to jammed cases and even, in extreme cases, casehead separations. This tendency is common to virtually all delayed-blowback weapons, but is minimised in the H&K designs by fluting the chamber so that the case is 'floated' on a cushion of gas to prevent it being forced too strongly out against the chamber walls. Heckler & Koch rifles have a good reputation for reliability and it is clear that the potential mischief that lies in the breech action is kept to an absolute minimum.

Apart from the provision of a bipod, which can be mounted either at the muzzle or in a rearward position immediately ahead of the magazine housing, the most obvious characteristic distinguishing the HK11 from the G3 is the heavyweight barrel (weighing 1.7kg). The barrel can be removed from the right side of the barrel casing once the retaining catch has been released. Instead of the angled-axis 100–400m backsight of the rifles, which rotates in a near-horizontal plane, the machine-guns have a 100–1200m drum which rotates vertically.

The original twenty-round detachable aluminium-body box magazines weigh 142g, compared with 1.62kg (empty) and 3.54kg (loaded) for the dual drum. The box magazines proved to be too flimsy and were supplemented, then replaced by steel-body patterns weighing about 288g empty (767g loaded). A 4x24 telescope sight with a 100–600m adjustment range can be fitted to a special mounting bracket attached to the left side of the receiver.

The original guns had selectors marked 'S' (*Sicher*, safe), 'E' (*Einzelfeuer*, single shots) and 'F' (*Feuer*, automatic fire), but newer versions are marked with multiple bullets.

Variants

HK11A1 This is a minor derivative of the HK11, easily distinguished by the design of the butt, which has a stepped under-edge to allow a left hand grip. A thirty-round magazine may be fitted instead of the standard twenty-round pattern.

HK11E Similar externally to its predecessors, this embodied important improvements. The barrel casing was lengthened, increasing sight radius in a bid to improve accuracy, and an additional three-round burst-firing unit was built into the trigger mechanism. A silent-closure system was provided for the bolt, a new three-position adjustable bipod was fitted and an optional NATO-standard optical sight bracket was provided. The sight and bracket added 650g to the weight of the gun. An auxiliary handgrip may be fitted beneath the fore-end to improve control when firing from the hip. The gun weighs 8.15kg with the standard box magazine and measures 1030mm overall, but can be fitted with a fifty-round drum **69**

magazine. Cyclic rate is usually listed as 700rds/min. The HK11E can be converted for sustained-fire roles – blurring the distinction with the HK21E (q.v.) – simply by substituting a belt-feed unit for the magazine housing and changing the bolt. Accessories include a slide-on winter trigger, a blank-firing barrel and a cleaning kit carried within the pistol grip.

Licensed production Guns of this type have been made in Greece by EBO. These are usually designated EHK11A1.

The HK11E, the most recent form of the HK11, has an elongated barrel casing, a three-round burst-firing capability, 'bullet' selector marks and an auxiliary fore-grip beneath the barrel casing.

Heckler & Koch HK12

Light-support machine-gun; HK-Maschinengewehr Modell 12
Made by Heckler & Koch GmbH, Oberndorf am Neckar
Specification HK12 light machine-gun
Data from a brochure dated October 1971
Calibre 7.62mm (.30)
Cartridge 7.62x39, rimless
Operation Delayed blowback, selective fire
Locking system Rollers delay the opening of the breech
Length 980mm
Weight 5.45kg (without bipod and magazine)
Barrel 450mm without flash-hider, polygonal rifling, right-hand twist
Feed Detachable twenty-, thirty- or forty-round box magazines, or eighty-round dual drum
Rate of fire 800±50rds/min
Muzzle velocity 750m/sec

Made only in very small numbers, this was a light-support version of the HK32 rifle, differing principally in the use of a heavyweight exchangeable barrel – weighing about 1.7kg – and in the magazines. Empty, these aluminium-body patterns weighed 140g (twenty rounds), 150g (thirty rounds) and 160g (forty rounds) respectively; filled weights were 500g, 690g and 880g. The plastic-body dual drum weighed 1.4kg empty and 2.83kg loaded. The backsight was the standard 100–400m rifle-type open drum instead of the 1200m pattern associated with most of the other H&K machine-guns.

Light-support machine-gun; HK-Maschinengewehr Modell 13
Made by Heckler & Koch GmbH, Oberndorf am Neckar
Specification HK13 light machine-gun
Data from a brochure dated October 1971
Calibre 5.56mm (.223)

Cartridge 5.56x45, rimless
Operation Delayed blowback, selective fire
Locking system Rollers delay the opening of the breech
Length 980mm
Weight 5.4kg (without bipod and magazine)

Barrel 450mm, polygonal rifling, right-hand twist
Feed twenty-, thirty- or forty-round detachable box magazines, or 100-round dual drum
Rate of fire 800±50rds/min
Muzzle velocity 970m/sec

The HK13 is a 5.56mm version of the HK11. Note the rifle-type backsight and how the length of the forty-round magazine hinders firing from cover.

Heckler & Koch machine-guns such as this 5.56mm HK13 are easily stripped down to their basic component groups. Note the twenty-round magazine, the detachable barrel and the roller set into the side of the breechblock (visible directly to the right of the barrel).

This is little more than a small-calibre version of the HK11, derived from the HK33 rifle, with a removable barrel and a rifle-type synthetic butt which reaches as far forward as the backsight base. The reduction of action length and the narrower magazine housing reduce overall length by about 5cm compared with the 7.62x51 guns. The standard rifle-type 100–400m open-drum backsight was fitted instead of the 100–1200m pattern associated with the HK11 and HK21 series.

The aluminium-body magazines weighed 113g (twenty rounds), 145g (thirty rounds) and 161g (forty rounds) empty, and 348g, 498g and 631g loaded. Figures for the drum were 1.35kg empty and 2.53kg loaded. The bipod added about 600g to the gun weight, and the 4x24 sight and its mounting bracket added another 650g.

The 5.56mm manufacturing pattern was subsequently changed to duplicate the HK11A1, though the designation does not seem to have been changed. The new-style gun has a heavier butt with a stepped under-edge, a special twenty-five-round box magazine and weighs about 7.7kg with its bipod. The empty magazine adds about 250g to this figure.

Variants

HK13C Dating from 1987, this is a minor variant of the standard HK13E with a baked-on camouflage finish – a mixture of beige, brown, green and dark grey/black.

HK13E This is a modernised version of the basic HK13 design, sharing the improvements made in the HK11E (q.v.). The barrel casing and the sight radius have been extended, an optional foregrip can be fitted and the three-round burst-firing capability has been built into the trigger system. A STANAG sight-mounting bracket can be attached to the receiver and a new twenty-five-round box magazine, weighing about 220g empty, has been standardised. The HK13E is 1030mm long and weighs about 8kg with its bipod, the detachable barrel/flash-hider assembly contributing 1.6kg to this total. The rifling makes a turn in 178mm, suiting it to the 62-grain SS109 5.56mm bullet.

HK13E1 Identical with the HK13E but for the rifling pitch, this is specifically intended to fire US 5.56mm M193 ball ammunition loaded with 54-grain bullets. The rifling makes a turn in 305mm.

HK13S Introduced in 1987, this is simply a variant of the HK13E with a baked-on desert sand finish, basically a sandy background with pale olive drab patching.

Heckler & Koch HK21 series
Germany

General-purpose machine-gun; HK-Maschinengewehr Modell 21
Made by Heckler & Koch GmbH, Oberndorf am Neckar
Specification HK21 GPMG
Data from a brochure dated October 1971
Calibre 7.62mm (.30)
Cartridge 7.62x51 NATO, rimless
Operation Delayed blowback, selective fire
Locking system Rollers delay the opening of the breech
Length 1020mm

Weight 7.3kg (without bipod)
Barrel 450mm without flash-hider, polygonal rifling, right-hand twist
Feed Metal-link belt
Rate of fire 850±50rds/min
Muzzle velocity 800m/sec

The HK21 is little more than a variant of the HK11 light machine-gun (q.v.), adapted to feed from a belt instead of a box magazine. It can be recognised by the horizontal feed tray, running through the receiver above and ahead of the trigger guard, which can handle DM1 fixed-link or M13 disintegrating-link belts (*see* MG 3, above) interchangeably. The French AAT 52-type belt can also be used.

The HK21 shares the 1200m drum sight of the HK11 and has the same design of butt and barrel casing. It can be converted to use box magazines simply by replacing the feed unit and changing the bolt, which blurs the distinction between the HK11 and HK21 still further.

Taken from rebel forces in Angola by the South African Defence Force, this well-worn HK21 was made in Portugal by FMBP in 1972.

The 7.62mm HK21A1, successor to the original HK21, is a belt-feed version of the HK11A1. Note the position of the feedway and the drum-type backsight. This particular gun has 'lettered' selector markings, but later examples have a simplified trigger/pistol-grip unit with 'bullet' markings.

Mounts included the HK 1100 tripod, which measured 770x570x230mm when folded and weighed about 9.2kg. The height of the bore in the firing position could be varied from about 350mm to 750mm. The mount allowed a traverse of 21.5 degrees either side of the centre line and a maximum elevation of 14 degrees; however, the cradle could be instantly disconnected from the training gear to allow all-round traverse under manual control. Other mounts included the HK 2400 pillar and an anti-aircraft/ground mount, designated HK 2700, which could also be adapted to suit the MG 3 or MG 42.

Variants

HK21A1 This is a minor upgrade of the HK21, with a stepped under-edge butt allowing a support-hand grip; on later guns, multiple-bullet markings replaced the 'S', 'E' and 'F' accompanying the original selector. Cyclic rate is 800rds/min. Like the HK21, the 21A1 version can be converted to use box magazines if required.

The standard HK21A1 could be easily altered to chamber the 5.56x45 round, by changing the barrel, the magazine and the bolt. The 5.56mm version weighs about 8.4kg and develops a muzzle velocity of about 840m/sec. Cyclic rate remains at about 800rds/min. The standard disintegrating-link belt has a

pitch of 10.6mm and weighs 103g empty or 691g loaded; a feed-tab adds 11g.

A 7.62x39 variant was also made, though the quantities involved are believed to have been very small; the call for Heckler & Koch weapons chambered for Soviet-style ammunition proved to be few and far between. The 7.62x39 HK21A1 weighed about 8.3kg and had a cyclic rate of 800rds/min. Muzzle velocity, however, was only 750m/sec. The fixed-link belt had a pitch of 12.7mm and the weight of a fifty-round example, with an integral feed tab, was 118g empty and 1013g loaded.

HK21E is an improved version of the HK21A1, offering the changes made in the HK11E (q.v.). These include an

An oblique view of an early HK21E, supplied to Franchi for trials in Italy, clearly shows the feed mechanism and the design of the backsight. This gun retains 'lettered' selector markings and lacks the auxiliary fore-grip often found beneath the barrel casing.

additional burst-firing capability built into the trigger mechanism, an extended barrel casing and a longer sight radius. Some guns were made with the standard 45cm barrel, but a brochure printed in October 1982 notes that the new 560mm pattern, weighing about 2.2kg, increased overall length to 1140mm; weight with the bipod became about 9.3kg. Cyclic rate is generally restricted to about 800rds/min. A box-magazine conversion unit is among the optional accessories.

Licensed production Guns of this type have been made in Greece by EBO.

These are usually designation EHK21A1. They have also been made in Portugal by Fabrica Militar de Braca de Prata of Lisbon, a division of Industrias Nacionais de Defesa de Portugal (Indep).

General-purpose machine-gun; HK-Maschinengewehr Modell 23
Made by Heckler & Koch GmbH, Oberndorf am Neckar
Specification HK23E light machine-gun
Data from a manual dated September 1987
Calibre 5.56mm (.223)
Cartridge 5.56x45, rimless

Operation Delayed blowback, selective fire
Locking system Rollers delay the opening of the breech
Length 1030mm
Weight 8.7kg with bipod
Barrel 450mm without flash-hider, polygonal rifling, right-hand twist

Feed Metal-link belt
Rate of fire 800±50rds/min
Muzzle velocity 915m/sec (SS109 bullet)

An improved form of the HK23A1, the HK23E has an extended barrel casing with an optional foregrip and an

The perfected version of the Heckler & Koch HK23E has a three-shot burst-firing capability built into the trigger system, requiring an additional setting on the selector. This gun also has the optional auxiliary fore-grip and the simplified trigger/pistol-grip unit with 'bullet' markings.

additional three-shot burst-firing capability built into the trigger system. The drum-type backsight is graduated 1–1000m, but a 4x24 optical sight and mounting bracket can be added at a cost of another 650g. The HK23E is rifled according to STANAG 4172, making a turn in 178mm for the SS109 bullet.

Variants

HK23A1 This seems to have been simply the small-calibre version of the 7.62x51 HK21A1 (q.v.), renamed to distinguish its chambering.

HK23C This is nothing but a version of the standard HK23E with a baked-on camouflage finish described above (*see* HK13C).

HK23E1 Outwardly identical with the standard HK23E, this is adapted for the US M193 bullet, its rifling making a turn in 305mm. Muzzle velocity is about 950m/sec, though cyclic rate remains about 800rds/min.

HK23S Dating from 1987, this is simply an otherwise standard HK23E with a desert sand finish, described under HK13S (q.v.).

HK73 This was little more than an HK23E adapted for the linkless feed system associated with the GR6, described below. The changes – not particularly successful – were abandoned after only a few guns had been made.

The 7.62mm HK23E mounted on its tripod to serve a heavy-support role. The belt-feed block is hinged down at the rear, but can be replaced with an adaptor (bottom centre) which accepts the standard G3-type box magazines (bottom left foreground) once the bolt (bottom left) has been exchanged.

Heckler & Koch GR6

Light-support machine-gun; HK-Maschinengewehr Modell GR6
Made by Heckler & Koch GmbH,
Oberndorf am Neckar
Specification GR6 light machine-gun
Calibre 5.56mm (.223)
Cartridge 5.56x45, rimless
Operation Delayed blowback, selective fire
Locking system Rollers delay the opening of the breech
Length 1030mm
Weight 8.04kg with bipod and empty magazine
Barrel 450mm, polygonal rifling, right-hand twist
Feed 200-round linkless-feed box or detachable box magazine with twenty-five rounds
Rate of fire 700±50rds/min
Muzzle velocity 950m/sec

Dating from 1983, this is a variant of the HK21E, described above, with an integral 1.5x optical sight adjustable for ranges of 100–400m. A laser designator may be built into the fore-end beneath the front sight. The GR6 can feed from a twenty-five-round steel-body box magazine, weighing 220g empty, but was originally conceived as part of a system involving a patented linkless-feed box holding 200 rounds plus ten held in reserve. Weighing 800g empty and 3.2kg loaded, this could be replenished with loose rounds or from ten-round chargers. A transparent backplate allowed the firer to assess the state of loading at a glance, but the system does not seem to have been efficient enough to attract widespread attention and the box magazines are customarily preferred.

Variants
GR6C A version of the basic gun with a camouflage finish (*see* HK13C).
GR6S Introduced in 1987, this is simply a minor variant of the GR6 with a baked-on desert sand finish (*see* HK13S).

General-purpose machine-gun; HK-Maschinengewehr Modell GR9
Made by Heckler & Koch GmbH, Oberndorf am Neckar
Specification GR9 light machine-gun
Calibre 5.56mm (.223)
Cartridge 5.56x45, rimless
Operation Delayed blowback, selective fire
Locking system Rollers delay the opening of the breech
Length 1030mm
Weight 8.74kg with bipod and empty belt box
Barrel 450mm, polygonal rifling, right-hand twist
Feed Metal-link belt
Rate of fire 800±50rds/min
Muzzle velocity 950m/sec

A belt-feed version of the GR6, this also shares its general construction. The integral 1.5x optical sight is retained and a laser designator may also be fitted in the fore-end. The belt box weighs about 740g empty and 3.5kg when loaded with 250 rounds in DM1 fixed-link or M13 disintegrating-link belts.

Variants
GR9C Dating from 1987, this is a version of the basic GR9 with a camouflage finish (*see* HK13C).
GR9S Essentially similar to the GR9C, this has a baked-on finish of desert sand design (*see* HK13S).

Light-support machine-gun
Made by Israeli Military Industries,
Ramat ha-Sharon
Specification Negev, long-barrel
version
Data from an IMI handbook dated July
1988
Calibre 5.56mm (.223)
Cartridge 5.56x45, rimless
Operation Gas operated, automatic
fire only
Locking system Rotating bolt
Length 1020mm (butt extended),
780mm (butt folded)
Weight 7.2kg with bipod
Barrel 460mm, six grooves, right-hand
twist
Feed Metallic-link belt
Rate of fire 725±75rds/min and
875±75rds/min (selectable)

Muzzle velocity 950m/sec with M193
ball ammunition

This is an interesting design, notable for
the use of a bifurcated piston rod and
twin return springs to provide a particularly compact envelope. It is easily
dismantled into six major components,
facilitating maintenance, and consists
largely of stampings and pressings in an

The Israeli 5.56mm Negev light machine-gun with its belt-bag.

The 5.56mm Negev makes a surprisingly efficient assault rifle once the bipod has been removed, the feed block supplemented by a box-magazine adaptor, and the short barrel substituted.

attempt to keep production costs as low as possible. Doubtless inspired by the FN Minimi (q.v.), sharing a similar rotating-bolt locking system, the Negev can be rifled for NATO or US-standard ammunition, the pitch of the grooves being a turn in 178mm and a turn in 305mm respectively. It fires from an open bolt, facilitating cooling, and has a gas-port provided with three settings, '1', '2' and '3': low power, high power, and closed to enable grenade launching. The cyclic rate varies with the gas-port setting.

Made largely of pressings and stampings, the Negev has a folding butt and an integral mount on the receiver for optical, electro-optical or thermal-imaging sights. The selector has three positions – automatic, single shot and safe. The safe position can be engaged even if the gun is cocked and also disconnects the trigger from the sear. Though the Negev is primarily intended to feed from standard feed belts, it can accept its own box and drum magazines, or the Galil or M16 box patterns once a suitable adapter has been fitted. The front sight is a post, adjustable for windage and elevation, whilst the

tangent-type aperture backsight is graduated from 300m to 1200m. A folding tritium night sight is also supplied. The gun can be fitted to most of the Israeli vehicle mounts, as well as the standard tripod.

Variant
Commando pattern This 330mm-barrelled gun can double as an assault rifle, particularly when box magazines are used and the bipod has been removed to save weight. It is 820mm long with the stock extended, or merely 650mm overall with the butt folded.

Light-support machine-gun; Arma di Squadra Mo. 70/78
Made by Pietro Beretta SpA, Gardone Val Trompia
Specification AS-70/78
Data from a Beretta leaflet, 1982
Calibre 5.56mm (.223)

Cartridge 5.56x45, rimless
Operation Gas operated, selective fire
Locking system Rotating bolt engaging receiver walls
Length 955mm
Weight 5.3kg with bipod
Barrel 450mm, four grooves, right-hand twist
Feed Forty-round detachable box magazine
Rate of fire 670rds/min
Muzzle velocity 970m/sec with M193 ball ammunition

The Beretta AS70/78.

The Beretta AS70/84 of 1984.

The first of Beretta's 5.56mm-calibre assault rifles, the AR-70 was soon adapted to provide not only a folding-stock carbine but also a light machine-gun. Introduced in 1979, the AS-70/78 shared the general construction of the rifles, but had a detachable barrel. This was locked in place by a pivoting latch on top of the front of the receiver ahead of the carrying handle, which, when lifted, allowed the barrel and the gas-port unit to be removed. The synthetic fore-end was attached directly to the barrel, but the bipod was mounted on the gas tube.

The AS-70/78 was moderately successful, but the detachable barrel and the resultant alterations in the design of the receiver lost the important commonality of parts with the assault rifle. Consequently, Beretta replaced the 70/78 with a simpler design.

The Beretta AS70/90 of 1985. Note the alterations in the butt, allowing an effective second-hand grip.

Variants

AS-70/84 The replacement for the 70/78 had a fixed heavy barrel, the trigger system being changed to allow the gun to fire automatically from the open-bolt position. The fore-end had distinctive diagonal slots and a bracket enabling a vehicle mount to be attached appeared under the action ahead of the box magazine, and the butt was a cutaway pattern with a folding shoulder strap. Only a few guns of this pattern were made before the 70/90 pattern was substituted.

AS-70/90 Dating from 1985, this perpetuated the general design of the 70/84, but the contours of the receiver are squared, the detachable carrying handle attaches to the backsight base, and the butt profile has been altered to facilitate a two-hand grip. The backsight is graduated 300–800m. Accessories include a laser aiming device, thermal imaging or electro-optical sights (the rail is a STANAG type), and a multi-piece cleaning kit carried in the pistol grip. Literature published in October 1985 gives overall length as 1000mm, with a 465mm barrel and a weight of 6.29kg (with bipod but without magazine). The six-groove rifling makes a turn in 178mm, cyclic rate being about 800rds/min. Most guns have been made with ambidextrous four-position selectors allowing single shots, three-round bursts and automatic fire in addition to a safety position.

Type 62   Japan

General-purpose machine-gun; 62-shiki kikanju
Made by Nittoku Heavy Industries Co. Ltd (NTK), Tokyo
Specification Type 62
Calibre 7.62mm (.30)
Cartridge 7.62x51 NATO, rimless
Operation Gas operated, automatic fire only
Locking system Tilting block
Length 1200mm
Weight 10.7kg with bipod
Barrel 524mm, four grooves, right-hand twist
Feed Metal-link belt
Rate of fire 600±50rds/min
Muzzle velocity 855m/sec

The Japanese, typically, have fitted the Type 62 with a locking system unlike anything else currently in production. The bolt is tipped as the piston/bolt carrier runs forward, but it rises at the *front* – not the back, as in the MAG and similar guns. The actual lock relies on two projecting lateral 'wings' on the breech-bolt rising into recesses in the receiver. Construction is complicated and the extraction system is unusual, but the guns operate reliably.

The Type 62 has a shoulder stock and an odd-looking pistol grip with a heel which projects from the under-edge of the receiver. The barrel is ribbed circumferentially (surprisingly widely apart) and a carrying-handle base, pierced to reduce weight, is attached to a barrel collar. The barrel can be removed simply by raising the top plate, depressing the latch and pulling the barrel handle forward. The Type 62 may be encountered on bipod or tripod mounts, though only about 3500 guns have been made and the Japanese Self-Defence Force (JASDF) has been forced to rely on additional supplies of US M60 machine-guns.

Variant
Type 74 This is a coaxial tank-gun variant of the Type 62, with a plain heavy 625mm barrel weighing 5.5kg (the standard pattern weighs 2kg). It may be fitted with spade grips and a mechanical or solenoid-equipped trigger system. The Type 74 is about 1085mm long and weighs 20.4kg.

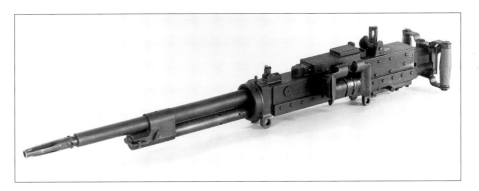

The Japanese Type 74 tank/vehicle machine-gun, shown here with spade grips and a mechanical trigger attached to the backplate, will also be encountered (often fired with a solenoid) fitted coaxially with the main armament of tanks and armoured cars.

Light-support machine-gun
Made by Daewoo Precision Industries
Ltd, Seoul
Specification K3
Data from maker's leaflet, *c.* 1988
Calibre 5.56mm (.223)
Cartridge 5.56x45, rimless
Operation Gas operated, automatic fire
only

Locking system Rotating bolt engaging
recesses in the barrel extension
Length 1030mm
Weight 6.85kg with bipod
Barrel 533mm, six grooves, right-hand
twist
Feed Thirty-round detachable box
magazine or 200-round belt
Rate of fire 850±150rds/min

Muzzle velocity 960m/sec with M193
ball ammunition

Basically a copy of the FN Minimi (q.v.),
the K3 has a solid-slab butt with a folding
shoulder plate. The fore-end has three
horizontal ribs to facilitate grip. A three-
position regulator is standard and, like its
Belgian-made prototype, the Daewoo
gun can be mounted on the US M122
tripod if the appropriate adaptor is
available.

The 5.56mm Daewoo K3 light machine-gun is little more than a copy of the Minimi.
Changes have been made to the design of the butt and fore-end, but the box-magazine
adaptor has been retained beneath the feed block and the operating system remains
largely unaltered.

CIS Ultimax M100 Mk III

Light-support machine-gun
Made by Chartered Industries of
Singapore Ltd
Specification Ultimax Model 100 Mark
III (U-100 Mk III)
Calibre 5.56mm (.223)
Cartridge 5.56x45, rimless
Operation Gas operated, automatic fire
only
Locking system Rotating bolt
Length 1024–1030mm, depending on
model
Weight 5.5kg (with bipod and empty
drum magazine)
Barrel 508mm, six grooves, right-hand
twist
Feed Detachable 100-round drum or
thirty-round box magazine
Rate of fire 500±100rds/min
Muzzle velocity 970m/sec with US
M193 ball cartridges

Advertised as 'the lightest of all light
machine guns designed at the outset for
one-man operation', the Ultimax is a
lightweight infantry-support weapon,
made largely of stampings and pressings
in a successful attempt to reduce weight.
The butt, fore-end/foregrip and pistol
grip are plastic injection mouldings, the
underside of the butt being shaped to

The 5.56mm Ultimax 100 Mark III, made in Singapore by CIS, can feed from a box magazine **(top)** *or a belt* **(above)**. *It is among the lightest guns in its class, but also amongst the most controllable thanks to its recoil-absorbing action.*

allow a European-style support-hand grip in automatic fire. However, the Ultimax is particularly easily controlled owing to the inclusion of an 'over length' recoil spring to allow the rearward movement of the recoiling parts to cease before they strike the inner back surface of the receiver.

This patented 'Constant Recoil' system gives an unusually low cyclic rate, but enables the gun to be fired without the 'jumping' that can characterise other lightweight guns of this type. Operated by a conventional short-stroke gas-piston system, the rotating bolt is locked by multiple lugs engaging the barrel extension.

The original guns, Mks I and II, had fixed barrels with the carrying handle midway along the receiver. The Mk III, however, has a detachable barrel. The bipod, which has telescoping legs, can be retracted and folded up along the sides of the fore-end. It is attached to the fore-end extension, allowing the barrel/ carrying handle/gas regulator group to be exchanged at will. The regulator has three positions to allow for variations in ammunition pressure.

The post-type front sight is an integral part of the gas-regulator housing, which means that changing barrels (Mk III only) does not compromise the sight line; the post can be adjusted by screwing it in and out. The backsight is an adjustable tangent-leaf design with a small peep, on top of the receiver immediately ahead of the butt. The leaf is customarily graduated to 600m, but can function for distances up to 1200m when raised vertically.

The cocking handle lies on the upper left side of the receiver, with a selector on the lower left side of the receiver above the pistol grip; the selector can be set by rotating the thumbpiece back (pointing to 'S') for single shots, or down to point to 'F' for fully automatic fire. Sling loops will be found on the left side of the fore-end cap and the left side of the detachable butt. Standard accessories include a cleaning kit, a sling, a 100-round drum magazine and the detachable bipod; optional extras include a 330mm barrel, a thirty-round box magazine, a bayonet lug, a blank-firing attachment and a selection of carrying pouches.

The Ultimax is a promising design, though, apart from adoption in Singapore, success has been confined to a few isolated purchases by Special Forces and anti-terrorist groups to whom its light weight and low recoil are attractive. However, whether it has the long-term durability to match the Belgian-designed Minimi (q.v.) is still moot.

Variants
In addition to the standard full-length gun, a short-barrel version has also been developed. This customarily lacks the butt and, therefore, can be carried in a surprisingly small package. A sound-suppressed barrel has also been developed experimentally.

CIS Fifty   Singapore

Heavy-support machine-gun
Made by Chartered Industries of
Singapore Ltd
Specification CIS Fifty
Data from a CIS leaflet dated June 1988
Calibre 12.7mm (.50)

Cartridge 12.7x99 (.50 Browning),
rimless
Operation Gas operated, automatic fire
only
Locking system Rotating bolt
Length 1670mm

Weight 30kg (without mount)
Barrel 1143mm, eight grooves, right-
hand twist
Feed Metal-link belt
Rate of fire 500±100rds/min
Muzzle velocity 890m/sec

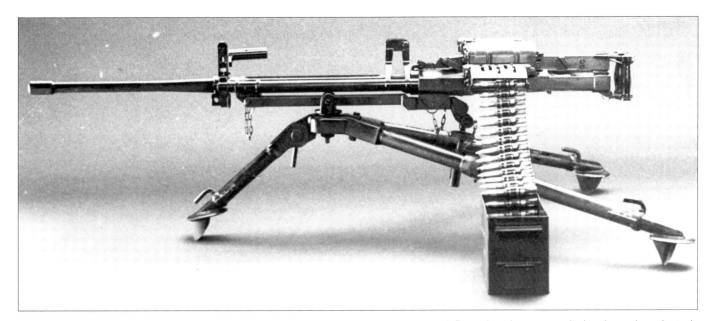

*The CIS Fifty is Singapore's answer to the problems most frequently solved by the .50 Browning. A compact design, it can be adapted
to fulfil differing roles.*

Introduced in 1988 to capitalise on the perennial popularity of the .50 Browning, this CIS design features a low cyclic rate and added controllability promoted by a modification of the Constant Recoil system pioneered in the 5.56mm Ultimax. This includes the provision of twin gas ports, on each side of the barrel block, which operate twinned piston rods and recoil springs. The CIS Fifty has a unique appearance, as the piston-rod tubes run back along each side of the readily detachable barrel. The sights are carried on brackets above the gas-piston tubes – possibly promoting zeroing problems – and each barrel has a sturdy handle. The backsight is a folding leaf pattern with a small peep.

The receiver is distinctively flat and broad, with spade grips and a charging handle on the right side beneath the right-hand feed block. Locked by rotating the bolt, the CIS Fifty fires from an open-bolt position and incorporates a safety sear to ensure that the gun cannot fire if it is dropped, jarred or mishandled when the chamber is loaded and the bolt is back. Important features of the design include the method of changing the barrel, which ensures that headspace remains constant, and the single-sprocket feed mechanism which can accept M15A2 disintegrating-link belts selectably from right or left. This gives the firer the option of switching between two belts loaded for different purposes – e.g., with standard ball or SLAP (Saboted Light Armor Penetrator) ammunition.

Mounts include the standard US M3 tripod, which requires a special adaptor, and pintles adaptable to shipboard or vehicle use. Optional extras include a flash-hider and a blank-firing attachment.

ALFA

Medium machine-gun; Ametralladora ALFA Modelo 44
Made by Fábrica de Armas de Oviedo
Specification ALFA 44
Calibre 7.9mm (.311)
Cartridge 7.9x57, rimless
Operation Gas operated, automatic fire only
Locking system Tipping breechblock engaging the receiver
Length 1450mm
Weight 13kg (40kg with tripod)
Barrel 750mm, six grooves, right-hand twist
Feed 100-round metal-link belt
Rate of fire 780±50rds/min
Muzzle velocity 760m/sec

An indigenous design, the ALFA machine-gun is a conventional air-cooled weapon with a conventional piston-type operating system. The breech is locked by tipping the tail of the bolt downward against a shoulder in the receiver floor. The gun has spade grips, with the trigger and safety lever on the receiver backplate. The rear portion of the barrel has circumferential fins to improve cooling.

Variants
Export version A derivative of the ALFA 44, supplied to Egypt in the early 1950s, may be distinguished by a jacket of aluminium cooling fins running the entire length of the barrel, larger slots in the gas cylinder and sights graduated in Arabic numerals.

ALFA 55 This is a derivative of the 44 model chambered for the 7.62x51 NATO cartridge. It is substantially shorter than the 7.92mm version – 1100mm overall, 610mm barrel – but develops a muzzle velocity of about 860m/sec.

The Spanish ALFA machine-gun. This is a 7.92mm 'export' example made in Spain for Egypt.

Light-support machine-gun
Made by Empresa Nacional Santa
Barbara, Madrid
Specification Ametralladora CETME
Modelo Ameli
Calibre 5.56mm (.223)
Cartridge 5.56x45, rimless
Operation Delayed blowback,
automatic fire only

Locking system Roller delay only
Length 970mm
Weight 6.71kg (7.24kg with bipod)
Barrel 400mm, six grooves, right-hand
twist
Feed Metal-link belt, 100 (standard) or
200 rounds (optional)
Rate of fire 1125±125rds/min
Muzzle velocity 875m/sec

The Ameli, externally resembling a
reduced-scale version of the German
MG 42/MG 3 series (q.v.), embodies the
delayed blowback roller-locking system
of the CETME rifle. It feeds from sealed
unitary belt-boxes, from the left, and has
a T-bar charging handle on the right side
of the receiver. The barrel can be
detached by unlocking its latch (which

*Resembling a miniature version of the German MG 42, the Spanish 5.56mm Ameli is derived from the CETME rifle and embodies the same roller-delayed breech mechanism. The guns may be mounted on a bipod for light support roles **(opposite)**, or on a special lightweight tripod if sustained fire is preferred **(above)**.*

doubles as the carrying handle) from the backsight block, rotating it 90 degrees sideways and withdrawing it from the right side once a section of the barrel casing has been hinged downward. The sights have tritium dots to improve performance in poor light. A rotating-disc element is built into the backsight block. Accessories include a special lightweight tripod mount, cleaning equipment,

optical and electro-optical sights, and a sling which can be used in conjunction with rings on the left side of the barrel casing and above the rear of the receiver immediately ahead of the joint with the butt. A cross-bolt safety catch runs through the pistol grip and the flash-suppressor has several rows of circular ports in addition to large lenticular cutouts.

Variant
Ameli 5.56-L This is a lightweight version of the basic gun, relying on extensive use of synthetic parts to reduce weight. The front sight folds back on top of the barrel casing and an M16-type flash suppressor is fitted. The basic Ameli-L weighs 5.2kg, and its lightweight bipod adds just 200g.

Vektor SS-77

South Africa

General-purpose machine-gun
Made by Vektor Industries, Pretoria
Specification SS-77, light-support
version
Calibre 7.62mm (.30)
Cartridge 7.62x51, rimless

Operation Gas operated, automatic fire
only
Locking system Displacement of the
bolt into the receiver
Length 1155mm, stock extended;
940mm, stock folded

Weight 9.6kg with bipod
Barrel 550mm, four grooves, right-hand
twist
Feed Metal-link belt
Rate of fire 750±150rds/min
Muzzle velocity 840m/sec

Sturdy and efficient, if heavier than some of its rivals, the 7.62x51 SS-77 is one of the most notable products of the modern South African small-arms industry.

An interesting, if somewhat conventional design, the SS-77 is another of many attempts to provide a gun that is light enough to be portable but heavy and durable enough to sustain fire for long periods. Development began in 1976, a prototype being followed in 1978 by three pre-production guns. The first phase of testing, completed in 1981, led to the ADM-1 (Advanced Development Model 1) in 1983 and the ADM-2 in 1984. The latter, with a few minor changes, was approved for production in the spring of 1986. The ADM-2 differed from the perfected SS-77 in the design of the folding butt, which was similar to that of the R4 (Galil) service rifle, and the fluting of the barrel, which was abandoned in favour of a plain-surface version shortly after series production began.

Externally elegant, but surprisingly heavy, the gun has a quick-detachable barrel and a side-folding butt to minimise overall length. The receiver is made from a machined forging, in very traditional style, while the furniture is nylon. The gun can still be fired with the butt folded or, alternatively, the butt can be replaced by a spade-grip backplate which will release the bolt even though the conventional trigger/pistol grip assembly remains in place.

Fixed-link DM 1 and disintegrating-link M13 belts will feed from the left, either from 100-round dustproof pouches or 200-round rigid boxes. Dust covers are provided over the feedway and the ejection slot, and a blade-type safety lever in the front of the trigger guard can be used to lock the trigger lever, the sear and the bolt in place. The backsight consists of a peep-block, a leaf and a ramp, suitable for 200–800m; the leaf can then be lifted vertically for distances of 800–1800m, a suitable aperture being provided in the slider. Tritium dots are provided to improve shooting in poor light.

The Vektor is gas operated, relying on lugs on the piston extension to cam the breechblock out of engagement in the receiver. This was based on the Soviet Goryunov (q.v.), which had proved its worth in the hands of insurgents in southern Africa. A bipod is standard, attached around the gas-piston tube and folding back into the underside of the fore-end, but the SS-77 can be adapted to a variety of tripods to act as a sustained-fire weapon. A range of optical, electro-optical, thermal imaging and laser-designating sights can be attached to an optional bracket on the side of the receiver when required.

Variant
Mini-SS Introduced in 1994, this is basically a 5.56mm conversion of the standard SS-77; a kit containing a new barrel, bolt, feed cover and gas-piston assembly can be supplied to order. The Mini-SS fulfils the role of a squad automatic weapon, particularly when fitted with a folding butt. It is about 1000mm long, weighs a substantial 8kg and has a 513mm barrel; six-groove rifling turns to the right. Muzzle velocity is about 980m/sec, cyclic rate being 800rds/min.

General-purpose machine-gun;
Maschinengewehr Modell 50
Made by Schweizerische Industrie-
Gesellschaft, Neuhausen am Rheinfalls
Specification MG-50
Calibre 7.5mm (.295)
Cartridge 7.5x55 M11, rimless
Operation Gas operated, automatic fire
only
Locking system Rollers in bolt body
Length 1270mm
Weight 16.8kg with bipod
Barrel 565mm, four grooves, right-hand
twist
Feed Fifty-round drum or 250-round
metal-link belt
Rate of fire 1000±100rds/min
Muzzle velocity 790m/sec

The MG-50 was a variant of the German MG 42. Made by SIG, largely by traditional gunsmithing methods, the guns were too expensive to sell in quantity. They were replaced by the simplified MG 710 series.

Developed to compete with the government-sponsored MG-51 (q.v.), this roller-locked weapon fed a continuous metal-link belt from left to right. It could be distinguished by a solid cylindrical receiver extension – carrying the bipod and backsight – which protected the gas port and piston assembly. The barrel could be changed easily, simply by releasing the locking latch and pulling the carrying handle forward. The MG-50 was not adopted in Switzerland, though the

Danish Army acquired small quantities in the early 1950s. These served as the *Maskingevær M51* until replaced in the 1960s by the Rheinmetall-made MG 42/59 (MG 3).

General-purpose machine-gun;
Maschinengewehr Modell 51
Made by Eidgenössische Waffenfabrik,
Bern
Specification MG-51
Calibre 7.5mm (.295)
Cartridge 7.5x55 M11, rimless
Operation Gas-assisted recoil,
automatic fire only
Locking system Pivoting flaps set into
the bolt
Length 1270mm
Weight 16kg without mount
Barrel 564mm, four grooves, right-hand
twist
Feed Fifty- or 250-round metal-link belt
Rate of fire 1000±100rds/min
Muzzle velocity 790m/sec

This was a simplified form of the wartime
German MG 42 (q.v.), relying on pivoting
locking flaps in the bolt instead of the
original rollers. The MG-51 was expensive
to make, being machined from high-
quality forgings, and was considerably
heavier than its German prototype. This
gave additional stability in the firing
position, despite an excessive cyclic rate.
Fitted on a 11kg tripod made to the same
high standards, the MG-51 served the
Swiss Army for many years.

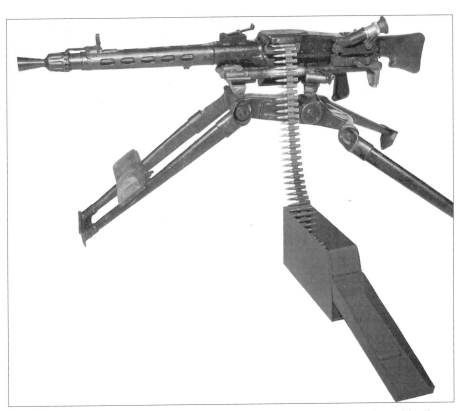

*The 7.5x55 MG-51, the standard Swiss GPMG until recent years, was adapted by the
Eidgenössische Waffenfabrik, Bern, from the wartime German MG 42 and retained the
same basic locked-breech concept.*

SIG MG 710 series

Switzerland

General-purpose machine-gun; Maschinengewehr Modell 710
Made by Schweizerische Industrie-Gesellschaft, Neuhausen am Rheinfalls
Specification MG 710-3
Details from a SIG brochure, 1972
Calibre 7.62mm (.30)

Cartridge 7.62x51 NATO, rimless
Operation Delayed blowback, automatic fire only
Locking system Delaying rollers on the bolt head
Length 1146mm
Weight 9.65kg (plus 0.7kg for bipod)

Barrel 560mm, four grooves, right-hand twist
Feed Metal-link belt
Rate of fire 875±75rds/min
Muzzle velocity 790m/sec

*The SIG MG 710-3, chambered for the 7.62x51 cartridge, is a variant of the German MG 42. Made only in comparatively small quantities, it will be encountered on a simple bipod mount **above** or on a buffered tripod **opposite**.*

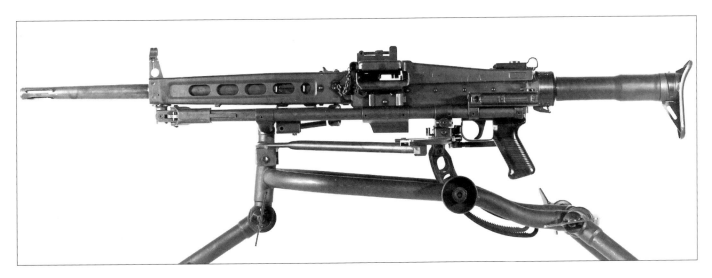

Also made in 6.5x55, 7.5x55 and 7.9x57, sold in small quantities to countries such as Bolivia and Chile, this simplified MG-50 – originally known as the MG-55 – embodies a delayed blowback breech locked by rollers engaging hardened-steel inserts in the receiver walls under the front of the feed tray. The design of the bolt and the bolt head ensure that the firing pin cannot reach the primer of a chambered round until the breech is properly closed. Ammunition belts, disintegrating or continuous, feed from the left side of the gun.

The receiver is made largely of pressings, and the oscillating-arm feed system

duplicates that of the original German guns. The barrel, which has a fluted chamber to minimise extraction problems, can be replaced simply by releasing the locking latch, though the design varied according to the pattern of gun.

Variants
MG 710-1 (MG-55-1) This has a full-length barrel casing like the MG 42 with the bipod mounted at the muzzle. The barrel can be removed by releasing the catch and pulling the breech sideways out of the right side of the casing. The backsight is mounted ahead of the feed cover.
MG 710-2 (MG-55-2) This gun has the

bipod mounted on a tubular extension of the receiver, which has three cooling slots on each side. The barrel can be removed by pulling it forward with the assistance of the carrying handle. The front sight still lies on top of the receiver ahead of the feed cover.
MG 710-3 Somewhat similar externally to the MG 710-1 but chambered only for the 7.62x51 cartridge, this has a slotted squared casing extending only a little over half the barrel length. The barrel can be changed by pulling it out of the right side of the barrel casing, then drawing it backward. Standard barrels weigh 2.04kg, compared with 2.5kg for a 101

heavyweight pattern and 1.89kg for the special blank-firing design. The sturdy 200–1200m tangent-leaf backsight lies on top of the feed cover, directly above the feed tray, while the front sight is attached to the barrel casing.

The MG 710-3 can be mounted on a bipod, which attaches to the underside of the barrel casing, or the SIG L-810 tripod. This has a buffered cradle attached to a horseshoe tube, which is in turn attached to the legs. The mount weighs 10.2kg, plus 400g for the sight bracket. Traverse is limited to 800mils (22°30′), elevation being 500mils (about 14 degrees). Firing height can be set for 300–700mm above ground level. A 2.5x Wild optical sight or a selection of infra-red sights can be attached to the tripod cradle, automatically aligning with the gun.

Accessories include a special chromium-lined 'long-life' barrel, ammunition drums and boxes, a blank-firing barrel, a spare barrel container, cleaning equipment, a sling and an ammunition-belt filler.

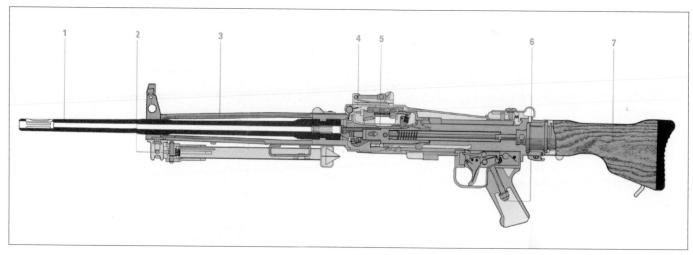

*A longitudinal section of the SIG MG 710-3. Key: **1** barrel, **2** bipod, **3** breech and barrel casing, **4** belt feed mechanism with feed apparatus lower part, **5** breech, **6** trigger, **7** butt with recoil spring.*

Light-support machine-gun; Squad Automatic Weapon
Made by the Hsing-Ho factory, Combined Service Forces Agency, Kaohsiung
Specification Type 75, standard version
Calibre 5.56mm (.223)
Cartridge 5.56x45, rimless
Operation Gas operated, automatic fire only

Locking system Rotating bolt engaging in receiver walls
Length 1050mm (approx)
Weight 6.9kg with bipod
Barrel 530mm (approx), six grooves, right-hand twist
Feed Metal-link belt
Rate of fire 800±50rds/min
Muzzle velocity 885m/sec

Rarely encountered in the West, this is little more than a variant of the FN Minimi, with alterations to suit Taiwanese manufacturing facilities. The country's principal general-purpose machine-gun is an indigenous variant of the US 7.62mm M60, designated Type 57.

The Taiwanese Type 75 Squad Automatic Weapon (SAW).

Ground, aircraft or vehicle machine-gun
Made by Colt's Patent Firearms
Manufacturing Co., Hartford,
Connecticut, and other
contractors
Specification M1919A4
Calibre 7.62mm (.30)
Cartridge 7.62x63 (.30-06), rimless
Operation Recoil operated, automatic
fire only
Locking system A rising block
engages a recess in the bolt
Length 1045mm
Weight 14.06kg (34.47kg with tripod)
Barrel 610mm, four grooves, right-hand
twist
Feed 250-round fabric belt
Rate of fire 500±50rds/min
Muzzle velocity 855m/sec

One of the best known of all machine-
guns, and also among the most
successful, this embodies an automatic
form of the rising-block lock introduced
on the Browning-designed Winchester
lever-action rifle of 1886. When the gun
fires, the barrel, barrel extension and bolt
recoil together; after travelling about
19mm, the locking block is pushed
downward to disengage its upper surface
from a slot in the underside of the bolt

The standard water-cooled .30 Browning M1917 on its tripod.

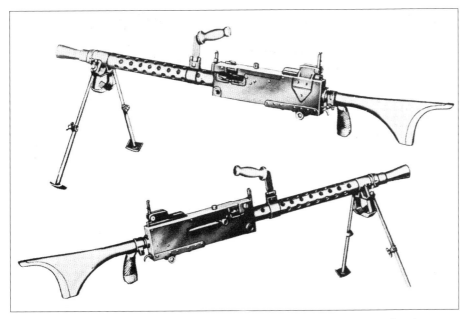

The air-cooled .30 Browning M1919A6. Note the strengthening plate riveted to the underside of the receiver ahead of the trigger.

body; barrel and barrel extension stop, allowing the bolt to run back alone, helped by the additional thrust imparted by a pivoting accelerator arm. A spring returns the bolt to join the barrel, stripping a new round into the chamber, and the bolt/barrel unit can finally run back into battery. As it does so, a cam shoulder in the underside of the receiver raises the locking block to re-engage the bolt.

Combat experience in the First World War soon showed the US Army that the M1917 Browning was an excellent design and it quickly replaced the Vickers Gun in front-line service. Production shortcuts left a weakness in the bottom of the receiver, but a reinforcing plate was simply welded on to surviving guns in the 1920s.

Adopted in 1936, the M1917A1 was an improved version of the original pattern. All the 1917-type service guns were eventually upgraded by replacing the old weak receiver bottom-plate with a strengthened pattern, improving the feed lever and the feed cover and re-calibrating the sights. Production of the M1917A1 continued throughout the Second World War, a steel water jacket replacing the bronze version in 1942 to conserve raw material. Declared obsolete in the 1950s, after sterling service in the Korean War, guns are still held in war reserve.

Variants
M1919A4 The A4 derived from trials dating back to 1924, when an experimental 24in barrel replaced the 18in pattern on an M1919A1, reducing the cyclic rate but improving the action. With the backsight on the cover plate and the front sight on the trunnion block and a greatly improved tripod, the M1919A4 was adopted to replace all the previous air-cooled guns. Most of the latter were subsequently converted to A4 standards. Ammunition belts fed from the left side of the breech.

The British Army still uses a few .30 M1919A4 Brownings, currently designated L3A3 and L3A4 (vehicle- and 105 tripod-mounted ground guns respectively) and others will be found throughout the world.

M1919A6 The result of tests held in 1942–3, this featured a shoulder stock and a bipod at the muzzle. This gun was very successful, though its considerable weight, which contributed greatly to its stability in sustained fire, did not endear it to the troops. Later examples had permanently mounted tripod adaptors, rotary carrying handles and synthetic furniture.

M2 aircraft gun The first Browning aircraft and tank guns were comparatively unsuccessful. In the early 1920s, therefore, a new aircraft gun was designed from scratch, with convertible feed and better synchronisation compatibility. Colt's Patent Firearms Manufacturing Company was permitted to exploit the project commercially in return for completing development, and the '.30 Aircraft Machine Gun, M2' was adopted in March 1931. Exceptionally successful in Britain during the Second World War – more than 70,000 were supplied under Lend-Lease – the M2 Browning was much less popular in USAF service, owing to a preference for the .50 version.

Mk 21 Mod. 0 This is the US Navy designation for a 7.62x51 conversion of the M1919A4 (*see* above).

M37 Classified as 'Standard A', this is a tank-gun version of the basic Browning design, with a retracting bar adapted from the M1919A4E1 pattern. It was used in fixed and flexible mounts. The M37C helicopter gun was similar, but had a solenoid-type trigger mechanism.

Licensed derivatives Fabrique Nationale and its successor, FN Herstal SA, have made large numbers of rifle-calibre Brownings in Belgium, in chamberings including .30-06, 7.65x53 and 7.9x57. The South African Vektor company is still making a 7.62x51 M4 in two versions, a fixed-mount CA gun for vehicles and aircraft, without sights or pistol grip, and a flexibly mounted AA pattern. These are newly made derivatives of old .303 British-type guns used in South Africa. The feed has been redesigned to use disintegrating-link belts, the guns firing from an open bolt, and a manual safety catch has been added.

Conversions Guns chambered for the 7.62x51 NATO cartridge have been made in some numbers in countries such as Australia and Brazil.

Browning, .50 series

Heavy-support, aircraft or vehicle machine-gun
Now made by Saco Defense, Inc., Saco, Maine
Specification M2 HB
Details for post-1978 Saco-made guns
Calibre 12.7mm (.50)

Cartridge 12.7x99 (.50 Browning), rimless
Operation Recoil operated, selective fire
Locking system Rising block engages a recess in the bolt
Length 1651mm

Weight 38.2kg (without mount)
Barrel 1010mm, eight grooves, right-hand twist
Feed Metal-link belt
Rate of fire 525±75rds/min
Muzzle velocity 853m/sec with M33 ball ammunition

A typical pre-1945 .50 Browning M2 on its tripod. Note the skeletal design of the carrying handle on the barrel, which distinguishes original-pattern guns from their modern QCB variants.

A detail view of a pre-1945 .50 M2 Browning machine-gun, fitted with a British Rank Pullin SS86 Crew Served Weapon Sight.

In April 1918, General Pershing, commanding the American Expeditionary Force (AEF), called for a machine-gun as powerful as the German 13mm-calibre 1918 pattern anti-tank rifle. Winchester developed a .50 cartridge, but performance proved disappointing and the project was abandoned until Frankford Arsenal produced a .50 cartridge simply

by scaling-up the .30 M1906 cartridge in May 1919.

John Browning had already successfully enlarged the .30 M1917 machine-gun for the Winchester .50 cartridge, but a hydraulic buffer had to be added to prevent the powerful Frankford round battering even the Browning to pieces. The water-cooled

.50 heavy machine-gun was standardised in 1921, though few had been purchased when the M1921A1 was substituted in 1930. This had a compound charging handle instead of a radial lever, the new handle being added to older guns when they came in for overhaul or repair.

An air-cooled gun was developed at

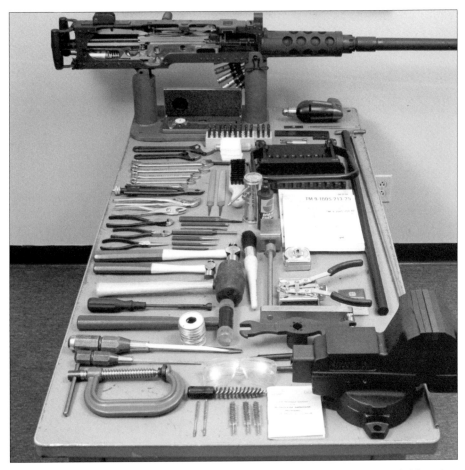

A sectionalised Ramo-made .50 M2 Browning, with the appropriate armourer's kit and training aids.

the request of the Cavalry Board in 1932, and the 'Caliber .50 Browning Machine Gun, Heavy Barrel, M2' was adopted in 1933. Finned barrels were abandoned before mass production began and the barrel length was increased from 36in to 45in in 1938, coincidentally slowing the cyclic rate and improving accuracy. Older guns were modified as they came in for repair.

The earliest .50 M2 aircraft guns had slotted barrel casings; later examples were simply drilled. Aircraft-gun parts will interchange with the M2 ground gun, except that the former always retained 36in barrels to maintain as high a cyclic rate as possible. In emergencies, aircraft guns can be used on ground mounts provided care is taken not to sustain fire for too long. All .50 Brownings had convertible feed, but almost always fed from the left when used on the standard tripods. Mounts currently include the M2 tripod, the M63 anti-aircraft mount and the M31 pedestal. A range of electro-optical, thermal imaging and laser designator sights can be fitted to the receiver when required.

A water-cooled M2 was developed to replace the M1921A1, with a new water jacket extending past the muzzle to cure the burn-out tendency of the earlier gun.

Production guns had spade grips if they were used in the ground or flexible airborne roles, or no grips at all if they **109** were fixed in vehicles or aircraft. Production of air-cooled M2 machine-guns during the Second World War totalled about 425,000 and there were about 82,500 water-cooled examples. Most of the latter, however, were converted to air cooling after 1945.

The M2 HB pattern remains the preferred heavy machine-gun of the US armed forces, partly because it has proved itself time and time again in combat but also because it fills a gap between rifle-calibre guns and the expensive and often sophisticated 20mm cannon. Saco Defense is currently the only accredited US manufacturer, the relevant specifications being settled in 1978. The guns retain the cumbersome barrel change system, however, which necessitates the use of time and a gauge to ensure that headspace is correct. Even though great advances have been made in the quality of .50-calibre ammunition, the ultra-short sight radius limits the advantages that can be taken. Guns can be set to accept belts from either side of the feed block.

Small quantities of the awesome .50 M2 HB Browning were purchased by the British Army in the 1970s, as 'Guns, Machine, Browning, 12.7mm L1A1' and placed in store; twenty-four of them were sent to the Falklands in 1982 where, on US M63 anti-aircraft mounts, they were used for local defence. They were so successful that studies have since been undertaken with a view to issuing L1A1 Brownings in an infantry support role. The guns' biggest drawback is simply their size.

Variants
Fifty/.50 This is a Saco development of the basic M2 HB. Extensive changes have been made to the receiver, which is an all-welded pattern and has a modified charging system and a detachable carrying handle attached to the barrel-support sleeve. The new cold-forged barrel, with an integral flash suppressor, can be exchanged merely by rotating the T handle and pulling it forward from the barrel-support sleeve, substituting a new barrel, then turning the barrel-handle back to its locked position. This avoids the headspacing problems common with standard M2 guns. Changes to the recoil buffer allow the cyclic rate to be varied at will (usually 500–750rds/min), allowing the gun to be switched from a ground role – where the low rate is preferable – to an anti-aircraft defence mode. The Fifty/.50 backplate has also been redesigned so that the spade grips are angled, making them more comfortable to hold and giving better access to the trigger.

The Fifty/.50 is 1560mm long and weighs about 25kg, saving about 35 per cent of the weight of the standard M2 HB. However, about 72 per cent of the components of the M2 HB are shared by the Fifty/.50 to retain as much commonality as possible.

M3 Attempts began in 1939 to increase the cyclic rate of the standard M2 – 800rds/min – and finally led to the greatly modified M3 (1200rds/min) in 1944. Though the M3 is superficially identical with the M2, few parts will interchange. The M3 remains in service, modern guns being fitted with Stellite barrel liners to increase bore-life.

XM213 A flexible-mount version of the M2 derived from the AN-M2 aircraft gun.

XM218 This was adapted for use specifically with the CH-47 helicopter.

Licensed versions The guns made by Fabrique Nationale and FN Herstal SA, owing to design changes, are covered separately in the Belgian entry.

M60 series   USA

General-purpose machine-gun
Made by Saco Defense Inc, Saco, Maine
Specification M60E1
Calibre 7.62mm (.30)
Cartridge 7.62x51 NATO, rimless
Operation Gas operated, automatic fire only
Locking system Rotating bolt engaging the receiver
Length 1105mm
Weight 10.51kg with bipod
Barrel 560mm, four grooves, right-hand twist
Feed Metal-link belt
Rate of fire 550±50rds/min
Muzzle velocity 865m/sec

The M60 light machine-gun was adopted in November 1956, though series production did not begin until 1960. Developed to replace all the Brownings excepting the vehicle guns, the M60 amalgamated a gas system whose origins lay in the Lewis (by way of Ruger's T10 and T23) with a belt-feed mechanism provided by the MG 42/T24. The action is locked by rotating lugs on the bolt head into the walls of the receiver, the gas piston and its extension being placed beneath the barrel. Like most machine-guns in its class, the M60 fires from the open bolt position to minimise cook-off problems.

The M60, however, had some severe faults of its own; the designers chose to fit the bipod on to the barrel rather than the gas-tube which, together with the carrying handle on the barrel casing

This view of a standard 7.62mm M60 machine-gun, being tried by a soldier of the King's Own Royal Border Regiment on an exchange mission at Fort Campbell, Kentucky, in 1978, clearly shows how the bipod is attached to the muzzle between the compensator and the front sight.

rather than the barrel, unnecessarily complicated barrel changing. In addition, the reliance on the backsight for zeroing meant that a barrel change could be accompanied by an appreciable change in impact-point unless the sights were adjusted. The M60 also had a poorly graduated backsight and sometimes generated too little power to lift lengthy ammunition belts.

However, in spite of the initial faults, the M60 series has been made in large numbers: by 1985, more than 250,000 had been made, for service with the armed forces of more than thirty countries. The guns are distinctive, with deep squared receivers ending in a butt plate with a hinged shoulder rest, and a deep ribbed fore-end ahead of the pistol grip. The carrying handle protrudes above the receiver, with the bipod on the barrel ahead of the front-sight bracket. A bracket for the belt-bag is attached to the left side of the breech. Most guns have barrels with chromium-plated bores and a Stellite liner to protect the mouth of the chamber from erosion.

The standard mount is the M122 tripod, though the Saco MSGH 60 may be used on vehicles, boats and helicopters. The backsight consists of an aperture block, operated by a finger wheel and an endless screw, which slides within a hollow pivoting leaf. However, laser designators and optical, electro-optical or thermal imaging sights can be fitted to mounting brackets attached to the right side of the receiver. These use a quick-clamp system which assures very little loss of zero when the sights are exchanged.

Variants
M60C The M60C is a stripped-down M60 with a solenoid-operated trigger and a hydraulic charger, widely used as a fixed gun on outboard helicopter mounts. These include the M23 for the

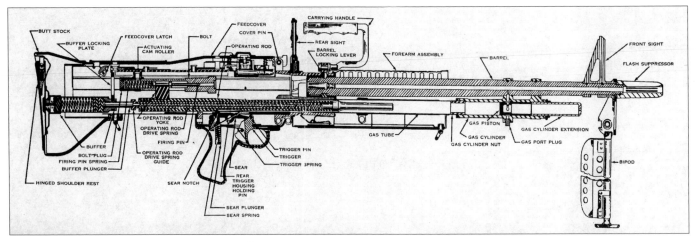

112 *A longitudinal section of the standard M60 machine-gun.*

UH-1D and UH-1H; M24 (door) and M41 (ramp) for the CH-47; and the M144 for the UH-60.

M60CA1 Classified as 'Standard B', this is an aircraft version of the M60C.

M60D Developed by Saco for use in the doorways of UH-1H and CH-47 helicopters, this is a much modified C with spade grips and a thumb trigger on the backplate. Also popular on ground vehicles and riverine craft, the M60D retains the bipod so that it can serve as a rudimentary local-defence weapon when removed from its pintle. The M60D is 1140mm long and weighs about 11kg.

M60E1 This included some of the obvious changes needed to improve the original M60, placing the bipod on the gas-tube and moving the carrying handle, but the guns are still regarded as inferior to the MAG and even the Russian PK in most countries outside the USA.

M60E2 Classified as 'Standard A' in 1977, and distinguished by changes to the gas system, particularly in the way gas was exhausted to the atmosphere, this was developed by Saco to equip the USMC M60A1 MBT (Main Battle Tank). It is distinguished by a cable-type charging system. Offered in two barrel lengths, the M60E2 measures either 1181mm or 1384mm overall and weighs 10.2kg or 11.1kg.

M60E3 Many observers felt that the role chosen for the M60 was much too wide,

Top *The US 7.62mm M60E2 machine-gun is intended for use in vehicles. It has a solenoid firing mechanism, a modified charging system and a tube beneath the barrel to extract exhausted propellant gas from the piston chamber.* **Centre and above** *This M60E3 ('Enhanced' 1993 version) shows how the basic M60 has been refined to provide a lighter gun. The provision of a foregrip and a belt-box bracket beneath the feedway makes the gun much easier to handle as shown by the soldier firing an M60E3 from the shoulder.*

113

as it had neither the mobility of a true light machine-gun such as the Bren Gun nor the sustained-fire capacity of the water-cooled .30 M1917 Browning. To improve the utility of the M60 in the light-support role, therefore, a lightweight version was developed. Capable of being fired from the hip whenever appropriate, the E3 was adopted by the USMC in 1983; by 1986, all existing Marine Corps M60 guns had also been converted to the same standards. Their most obvious features are the straight-comb butt, the lightweight barrel, a bipod attached to the gas-piston tube which folds back alongside the barrel, and an auxiliary

fore-end pistol grip. Sling swivels lie on the left side of the bipod-attachment block and on the left side of the butt. The standard M60E3 is 1077mm long and weighs 8.8kg; however, an optional short barrel reduces the length to 940mm and the weight to 8.7kg, whilst a full-length heavy barrel, intended for sustained fire for longer periods before removal, raises the weight to 9.4kg.

The feed cover can be closed regardless of whether the bolt is open or closed, a 'winter' trigger guard can be snapped downward to allow a gloved finger access to the trigger lever, and a skeletal support bracket for the belt-bag

is attached to the left side of the receiver. A locknut on the gas cylinder allows easy access for cleaning and the piston is designed to be reversible to prevent misassembly. A conversion kit can be obtained to allow earlier M60 guns to be converted to M60E3 standards when required.

M60E4 An improved form of the E3 pattern, with an integral sight mounting rail, a short barrel and an improved gas-regulation system, this dates from 1994. It is competing against the M240E4 (a modified FN MAG) for adoption to replace the M60.

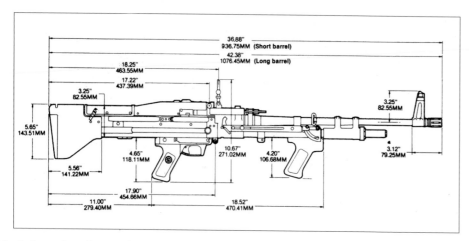

114 *A dimensioned general-arrangement drawing of the M60E3.*

GEC M134/GAU-2B Minigun

USA

Motor-driven machine-gun
Made by the Armament Systems
Division of General Electric Company,
Burlington, Vermont
Specification M134
Calibre 7.62mm (.30)
Cartridge 7.62x51, rimless
Operation Externally powered,
automatic fire only

Locking system Rotating bolt
Length 802mm
Weight 16.3kg (gun only)
Barrel 560mm, four grooves, right-hand
twist
Feed Disintegrating metal-link belt or
linkless feed
Rate of fire Up to 6000rds/min
Muzzle velocity 920m/sec

Derived from the Gatling Gun by way of
experiments beginning shortly after the
end of the Second World War (*see*
Introduction), this relies on a cluster of
six barrels locked by a 180-degree turn
into a rotor assembly supported in the
'receiver' or gun-housing by ball bear-
ings. The barrels are held in place by
clamp discs, allowing them to be fitted

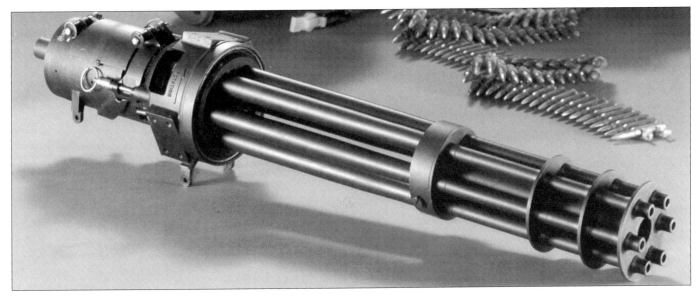

A six-barrel 7.62mm Minigun.

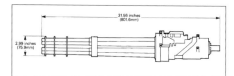

A dimensioned general-arrangement sketch of the 7.62mm GEC Minigun emphasises its compact construction.

either parallel or convergent at a pre-set distance.

Each barrel is accompanied by a bolt, which can be rotated to lock into the barrel extension by a cam track cut in the rotor. Each track contains a firing cam, which retracts and then releases the striker, and a dwell-path which ensures that the bolt remains locked until the projectile is well clear of the muzzle and the gas pressure in the chamber has dropped to a safe level.

Pressing the firing button starts the barrel cluster rotating anticlockwise (viewed from the rear) and a roller on each bolt follows its own cam track, successively picking up a live round from the fingers of the guide bar; ramming the cartridge into the chamber; locking the bolt; firing the gun, then opening the bolt again to extract and eject the spent case. Feed is customarily from 4000 linked rounds in a container, helped by a plastic chute running up to the gun. An auxiliary

116 feed motor can be provided if the chute is

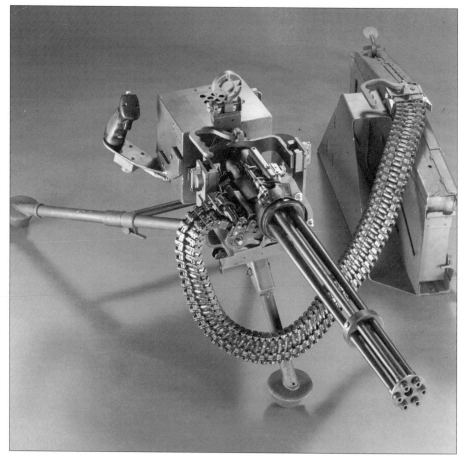

A six-barrel 5.56mm XM214 SixPak Minigun mounted on a tripod for a support-fire role. Note the feed box and conveyor.

particularly long or its curves are unusually tight, though the Miniguns have an enviable reputation for reliability – any cartridges that misfire are simply extracted and thrown clear of the gun, causing problems only in the event of a hangfire.

Variants

5.56mm Minigun Another of the six-barrel designs, this measures 731mm overall and weighs about 10.2kg. Miniguns are particularly compact in relation to their power and the breech housing of the 5.56mm version is just 220mm long. The rate of fire can be varied between 400rds/min and 6000rds/min. Gun life has been estimated as 500,000 rounds, owing to the reduction in operating stresses by the use of multiple barrels and an external power source.

.50-calibre Minigun (Gecal 50, GAU-19/A) Offered in three- or six-barrel configurations, with fire-rates as high as 4000rds/min and 8000rds/min respectively, with a 'time-to-rate' of just 0.3 seconds, these powered Gatlings can be adapted to airborne, land or naval requirements. The guns will handle ammunition ranging from conventional ball and armour-piercing patterns to the latest SLAP and fused HEI (High Explosive Incendiary) designs. Drive can be electric, hydraulic or pneumatic. It is even possible to acquire a self-starting drive system utilising propellant gas, for use where external power is not available. The guns are 1180mm overall, with the standard 914mm barrel, and weigh 30kg (three-barrel) or 43.6kg (six-barrel) without mounts or accessories. Muzzle velocity is about 885m/sec, though this increases somewhat if long-barrel (up to 51in) options are selected. The optimal fire-rates are customarily set at 1000rds/min for three-barrel guns and 2000rds/min for six-barrel guns.

Above A six-barrel .50 Minigun. Note its surprisingly compact dimensions in relation to the helmets.

Left A three-barrel .50 GEC Minigun demonstrates its awesome capabilities on a vehicle mount. It is quite obvious from the muzzle blast that the firing barrel is in the lowest position.

M73 series

Tank/vehicle machine-gun
Made by Rock Island Arsenal, Rock Island, Illinois, and the General Electric Company, Burlington, Vermont
Specification M73, standard version
Calibre 7.62mm (.30)
Cartridge 7.62x51 NATO, rimless
Operation Recoil operated, automatic fire only
Locking system Laterally moving block
Length 889mm
Weight 14kg
Barrel 559mm, four grooves, right-hand twist
Feed Metal-link belt
Rate of fire 575±50rds/min
Muzzle velocity 854m/sec

Designed by Colby and Lockhead of General Electric and standardised in 1959, this was an attempt to replace the venerable .30 and .50 M2 Brownings, plus the .30 M37 and M37C (variants of the M1919A5 with improved headspace, the latter with solenoid trigger and hydraulic charging).

The M73 relies on a small sliding breechblock and an independent rammer mechanism to feed cartridges into the breech. When the barrel recoils, the locking block is moved to the right by

a lug on its base working in a cam path in the breech. The guns normally feed from the left, but can be adapted if required to feed from the right. Unfortunately, the complexity of the locking/extraction/ejection cycle, a consequence of seeking an ultra-compact receiver, required a special carrier to be provided beneath the breech. Though the 2.4kg M73 barrel can be changed extremely easily, merely by rotating the receiver to either side to give access to the breech, the basic design was not successful enough to remain in service for a long period.

The M73 vehicle gun was compact, but comparatively unsuccessful.

Variants
M73C This had a flash suppressor rather than a flash-hider.
M73D An experimental tripod-mounted ground gun with a distinctive 'saw grip'. Comparatively few were made, though some saw active service in Vietnam.
M219 Dating from 1970, this was a revised version of the M73, intended to cure the faults that had become apparent in service. Extensive changes were made in the rammer and feed mechanism, and the timing of the operating cycle was changed by revising the cam path. Yet the M219 proved to be little better than its predecessor and was itself replaced by the M60E2 in the 1980s.

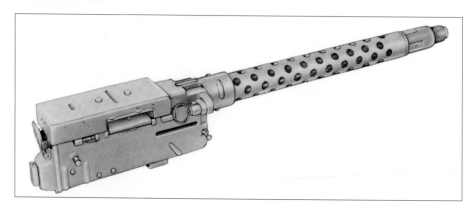

Stoner XM207E1

Light-support machine-gun; also known as the Stoner M63A1
Made by the Cadillac Gage Corporation, Warren, Michigan
Specification XM207E1
Data for belt-feed version
Calibre 5.56mm (.223)
Cartridge 5.56x45, rimless
Operation Gas operated, selective fire
Locking system Rotating bolt engaging the receiver
Length 1022mm
Weight 5.65kg with bipod

Barrel 551mm, six grooves, right-hand twist
Feed Metal-link belt
Rate of fire 700±75rds/min
Muzzle velocity 990m/sec

The adoption of the 5.56mm cartridge inspired the development of several systems in which basic components could be assembled to provide a range of weapons from a submachine-gun up to a tripod-mounted belt-fed infantry-support weapon. Made firstly by the Cadillac Gage

Company and then licensed to NWM, the Stoner system used a standard pistol-gripped receiver unit that could be assembled in several combinations – an assault rifle, a carbine, a light machine-gun with top-mounted box feed, a similar gun with belt feed, a belt-feed infantry-support machine-gun mounted on a tripod, and even a stripped-down vehicle gun. All relied on a simple gas-operated rotating bolt lock and encountered limited success when the XM207 light machine-gun was purchased in small numbers for

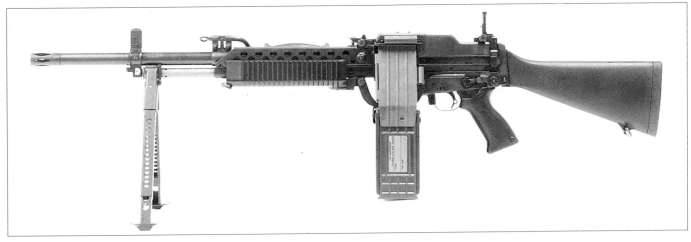

Stoner M63A, with feed cover closed.

Stoner M63A, with feed cover open. Capable of being configured as a machine-gun, an assault rifle or a carbine, the Stoner M63 was a brave effort to provide a weapons system. The 5.56mm XM207 was unsuccessfully evaluated by the US Army as an infantry-support weapon, though small quantities were purchased by the Army and Navy for Special Forces use.

the US Special Forces.

Service use showed that the Stoners were somewhat lightly made and prone to jamming if not carefully maintained; however, the consensus was that the faults could be overcome if funding was available. Ultimately, the US Army decided to retain the M16A1 and the Stoner weapon system was abandoned. Like all such efforts, Stoner's failed partly because of pitfalls from trying to be a jack of all trades and partly because the 5.56mm round (a compromise, after all) is too powerful for a submachine-gun while offering insufficient long-range performance to replace guns such as the M60.

Variant

Mk 23 Mod. 0 This was the US Navy designation for the XM207E1, used in small numbers by the SEAL teams in the 1960s and 1970s.

General-purpose, aircraft and vehicle machine-gun
Made by FN Manufacturing, Inc., Columbia, South Carolina
Specification M240G
Calibre 7.62mm (.30)
Cartridge 7.62x51 NATO, rimless
Operation Gas operated, automatic fire only

Locking system Displacement of the bolt-tail into the receiver
Length 1220mm
Weight 11.7kg with bipod
Barrel 627mm, four grooves, right-hand twist
Feed Metal-link belt
Rate of fire 750±50rds/min
Muzzle velocity 853m/sec

This is little more than a US-made version of the FN MAG pictured and described in detail in the Belgian entry. Classified as 'Standard A' in 1977, the XM240 replaced the M73, M73A1 and M219 tank/vehicle guns, which had proved to be inefficient. It was characterised by left-side feed.

Variants
M240C This was simply an M240 with right-side feed.
M240E1 A derivative of the standard tank/vehicle version, the first of these was delivered in the spring of 1988. Intended for flexible use, the guns have mechanical triggers and spade grips mounted on the backplate.
M240E4 Submitted in 1994 to the US Army Advanced Medium Machine Gun Program (AMMP), this derivative of the M240E1 offers an integral sight mounting rail, a conventionally shaped synthetic butt and a barrel guard/fore-end assembly perforated with ventilation holes. An M16A2-type flash suppressor is used.
M240G Standardised by the USMC in 1995, this is similar to the 240E4, with a shoulder stock. It is intended to be issued with either bipod or tripod mounts, depending on the role envisaged for individual guns.

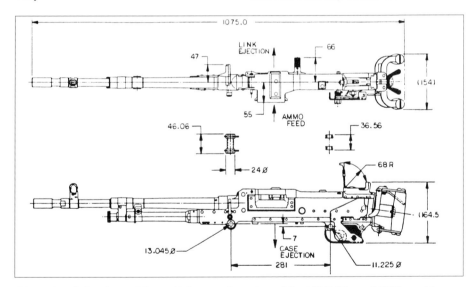

Dimensional drawings of the vehicle-mount version of the US 7.62mm M240 machine-gun. Measurements are in millimetres.

M249 SAW USA

*Light-support machine-gun; Squad
Automatic Weapon*
Made by FN Manufacturing, Inc.,
Columbia, South Carolina
Specification M249, light-support
version
Calibre 5.56mm (.223)
Cartridge 5.56x45, rimless
Operation Gas operated, automatic fire
only
Locking system Rotating bolt
engaging in receiver walls
Length 1040mm
Weight 6.85kg with bipod
Barrel 523mm, six grooves, right-hand
twist
Feed Detachable thirty-round box
magazine or 200-round metal-link belt
Rate of fire 750±50rds/min
Muzzle velocity 885m/sec

Adopted as 'Standard A' in 1982, this is a
US-made variant of the Belgian Minimi
(q.v.). Orders for 50,000 US Army and
10,000 USMC guns were suspended in
1985 pending the resolution of problems
encountered with the first series batches,
leading to the introduction of a 'Product
Improved' version in 1987.

    The perfected 5.56mm M249, like the
essentially similar Australian F89, has a

conventional synthetic butt instead of the
original tubular type. A new recoil buffer
was fitted; a heat shield was added
above the barrel; a collapsible carrying
handle replaced the fixed type; the
adjustable gas regulator was replaced by
a fixed design; and an M16A2-type flash
suppressor was used.

*The 5.56mm M249 is the standard US Army light machine-gun. It is a minor variant
of the Belgian Minimi, retaining the dual-belt/box-feed system, but has a solid butt and
other detail differences. The guns are being made in the USA in large numbers.*

Ares

Light-support machine-gun
Made by Ares, Inc., Port Clinton, Ohio
Specification Ares 556 LMG
Calibre 5.56mm (.223)
Cartridge 5.56x45, rimless
Operation Gas operated, selective fire
Locking system Rotating bolt
Length 1073mm (butt extended),
971mm (butt retracted)
Weight 4.91kg with bipod and
lightweight barrel (belt-feed pattern)
Barrel 550mm including flash-hider, six
grooves, right-hand twist
Feed Metal-link belt
Rate of fire 600±50rds/min
Muzzle velocity 945m/sec

One of the unsuccessful competitors in the US Army's Squad Automatic Weapon (SAW) competition, development of the Ares has been continued in the hope of attracting export orders and it has since been made in small quantities on a batch-by-batch basis. The Ares has a conventional gas-piston system and is locked by a rotating bolt. The barrel is a quick-detachable type, requiring no elaborate headspacing adjustments. Machine-guns are usually supplied with a belt-feed mechanism, but can accept standard M16 magazines if a suitable adaptor is fitted; unusually, these feed downward from the left side of the attachment block.

One of the most significant advantages of the Ares lies in its weight; fitted with a lightweight barrel and a box magazine, it weighs less than 4.5kg (10lb). Published figures indicate a weight of 8.51kg with the bipod and a full 200-round M249 feed box. The standard barrel assembly weighs 1.73kg, the bipod contributing 560g to the total. Overall length without the detachable butt is 813mm. The gun has an M16-type pistol grip, and a vertically ribbed fore-end with circular cooling holes directly above the barrel.

The finalised guns (but not the prototypes) have seven circular holes through the sight rib on top of the rear receiver, reducing weight without sacrificing rigidity. Some guns are rifled with a one-in-seven twist for the M855 bullet; others retain the one-in-twelve twist for the M193 bullet, though this is considered to be optional.

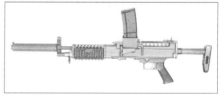

*The 5.56mm Ares competed unsuccessfully in the US Army SAW trials, but was deemed to have sufficient commercial potential for development to continue. The gun is normally encountered with a short tubular butt and a bipod **top**, but can be configured with a short barrel and a sound moderator **above**. Belt or box-magazine feed is optional. The box is inverted on the left side of the breech, which is unusual for a modern design, although popular prior to 1945.*

EX-34 Chain Gun

Motor-driven aircraft/vehicle gun
Made by Hughes Helicopters, Inc.,
Culver City, California
Specification EX-34, standard
configuration
Calibre 7.62mm (.30)
Cartridge 7.62x51 NATO, rimless
Operation Externally driven, automatic
fire only
Locking system Rotating bolt
Length 940mm
Weight 13.7kg
Barrel 559mm, four grooves, right-hand
twist
Feed Metal-link belt
Rate of fire 1-600rds/min
Muzzle velocity 835m/sec

This is a very interesting design,
conceived in the summer of 1972 as a
30mm cannon. Rechambered in 1976 for
the standard 30mm DEFA/ADEN
ammunition, the M230 and its linkless
feed were approved for the AH-64
Apache helicopter. The success of the
combination persuaded Hughes to
reconfigure the Chain Gun for rifle-calibre
cartridges in the 1980s.

The EX-34 relies on an electrically
driven endless roller chain in the breech,
which, by way of a shoe and cam

mechanism, controls the movement of
the bolt and fires the gun. Cartridges are
fed from an independently powered belt
drive. Characterised by simple and
sturdy construction, the Chain Gun fires
from the open bolt position, the unusual
length of the bolt-lock dwell preventing
gas fumes seeping back into a vehicle
through the open breech.

Used in Britain, Canada and
elsewhere in addition to the USA, the
Chain Gun is an ideal helicopter/vehicle
gun, owing to its ultra-compact design.
The barrel can be changed in a few
seconds and the EX-34 will interchange
with the M60E2 in standard US coaxial

mountings. These particular Chain Guns
have full-length barrel jackets, with
venturi-type evacuators, and eject their
spent cases externally.

British guns, designated L94A1, have
been made by the Royal Small Arms
Factory in Enfield and by its successor,
Royal Ordnance plc, in Enfield and
Nottingham. The L94 has a 703mm
Stellite-lined barrel, measures 1250mm
overall, and weighs about 17.9kg; cyclic
rate is restricted to about 500rds/min. A
mount on the barrel jacket suits it to the
Challenger II main battle tank and the
Warrior AFV.

*The Hughes 7.62mm EX-34 Chain Gun presents a different approach to machine-gun
design which has resulted in a very compact weapon ideally suited to vehicle or airborne
use. Guns of this type are now being made in Britain under licence.*

DPM series

Light-support or vehicle machine-gun;
Pulemet Degtyareva Pekhotniy
Moderniizirovanniy
Made by the Kovrov machine-gun factory
Specification DPM, standard infantry
version
Calibre 7.62mm (.30)
Cartridge 7.62x54, rimmed
Operation Gas operated, automatic fire
only

Locking system Pivoting flaps set into
the bolt
Length 1270mm
Weight 9.8kg with bipod
Barrel 605mm, four grooves, right-hand
twist
Feed Detachable pan magazine with
forty-seven rounds
Rate of fire 600±50rds/min
Muzzle velocity 840m/sec

Introduced during the Second World War,
this was an improved version of the
original Degtyarev-designed DP light
machine-gun of 1927. The DP had been
made in large numbers prior to 1941, in
infantry, tank and aircraft versions, but
the need to concentrate on production
engineering forced the Soviet authorities
– though well aware of the situation – to
overlook serious teething troubles with

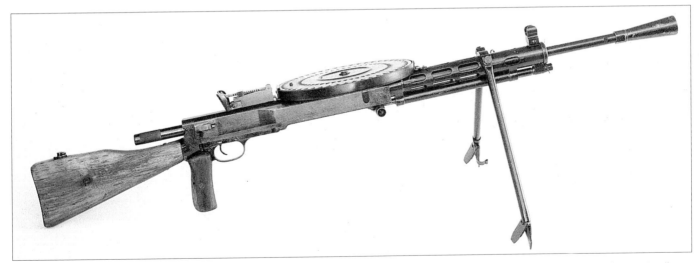

The Soviet 7.62mm DPM was introduced in 1944 to replace the DP. The separate pistol grip and the return-spring housing protruding
from the back of the receiver distinguish it from its predecessor.

their new machine-guns. Trials were undertaken throughout the 1930s, but not until the Second World War had almost run its course were changes made.

Adopted in August 1944 and customarily credited in Soviet sources to V. Shilin, the DPM shared the basic operating system of the DP, with a cumbersome pan-type magazine (1.65kg empty, 2.83kg loaded) above the receiver. Locking flaps in the breech were forced outward into the receiver walls as the firing pin flew forward to strike the primer of a chambered cartridge. A three-position adjustable gas regulator ensured acceptable reliability in adverse conditions, though excessive friction due to the broad bearing surfaces in the action promoted stoppages and misfeeds.

The most obvious change concerned the position of the return spring, which, originally beneath the barrel, was moved to a tubular housing that protruded from the rear of the receiver above the wrist of the butt. This prevented heat from the barrel weakening the spring, but had been tried in the early 1930s! The firing mechanism was improved, a radial safety lever was added on the right side of the receiver to replace the original grip pattern and a pistol grip was added behind the trigger guard. The original detachable bipod was replaced with a captive pattern, which, however, could **126** rotate around the longitudinal axis

A tank gun, the DTM, was also made in quantity; this lacks all but the most rudimentary sights and has a compact two-tier pan magazine.

provided by the slotted barrel casing.

The gun had a tangent-leaf backsight on the receiver, behind the pan magazine, and a tubular charging handle protruding beneath the lower right side of the receiver. A large conical flash-hider was attached to the muzzle and there were sling loops on the left side of the barrel casing and the butt.

Production seems to have been substantial, but it was recognised that the pan-type magazine limited sustained-fire capabilities too much; Degytarev had submitted a belt-fed adaptation of the DP in 1943 and it is suspected that the DPM was little more than a stopgap pending the development of better weapons (*see* RP-46).

Variants

Type 53 This was a version of the standard Soviet-type DPM made in the People's Republic of China. It can be identified by its markings, which include ideographs on the receiver signifying 'Type 53'.

DTM The tank and armoured-vehicle version of the DPM replaced the earlier DT with effect from 1 January 1945. Capable of being mounted on a pillar or in an armoured ball, the DTM had a folding backsight. It was essentially similar to the infantry pattern, but had a two-tier pan magazine and a retractable butt with a shoulder strap. The butt components were made from stampings in an attempt to save production time. Some guns were fired electrically, a suitable solenoid and a trigger-actuator being attached to the front of the pistol grip beneath the trigger guard.

DShKM USSR

*Heavy-support or vehicle machine-gun;
Stankoviy Pulemet Degtyareva-Shpagina
Krupnokaliberniy Modernizirovanniy*
Made by the Kovrov machine-gun
factory
Specification DShKM, standard pattern
Calibre 12.7mm (.50)
Cartridge 12.7x108, rimless
Operation Gas operated, automatic fire
only
Locking system Pivoting flaps set into
the bolt
Length 1588mm
Weight 35.7kg (gun only)
Barrel 1070mm, eight grooves, right-
hand twist
Feed Fifty-round metal-link belt
Rate of fire 575±25rds/min
Muzzle velocity 860m/sec

This has its origins in the unsuccessful DK
machine-gun developed in 1929–31 after
the failure of guns based on the .5 Vickers
cartridge to prosper in Soviet Army trials.
The DK was locked by a variant of the
flap-lock system embodied in the DP,
actuated by the firing pin, and fed from a
thirty-round drum magazine. However,
inability to sustain fire for long periods and
a low cyclic rate contributed to its
downfall. The answer to the problem was

*The DShK heavy machine-gun, introduced in 1938, was distinguished by a prominent
rounded feed-cover above the breech. Made in large numbers during the Second World
War, guns of this type soldiered on into post-war days. The 1946 modification, creating
the DShKM, substituted a conventional belt-feed mechanism for the sprocket-type
Shpagin unit.*

found by Georgiy Shpagin, who developed an indexing block, mounted on top of the receiver beneath a curved sheet-steel cover, which enabled a metal-link belt to be substituted for the Kladov drum. The motion of the bolt carrier was used to revolve the feed block by way of an intermediate rocking lever mounted on the right side of the receiver, and a three-position gas regulator was provided to assure reliability in adverse conditions.

Adopted in February 1939, the DShK proved to be much more reliable than its predecessor and was capable of sustaining fire for long periods. Its barrel weighed a substantial 12.7kg. The backsight could be raised vertically and the standard mount was the 1938-pattern tripod; the mount was supplied with detachable wheels and an optional armoured shield for use in ground roles. The gun fed from a closed-pocket metal-link belt, individual cartridges being withdrawn backward before being rammed into the chamber. An assortment of high-angle anti-aircraft sights was provided and, from 1943, guns of this type were mounted on the turrets of the first IS-2 tanks.

The DShK worked well enough, but the Shpagin feed system could only operate if the belts were fed from the left. This restricted the use of the heavy machine-guns in aircraft and multiple mounts. Consequently, in 1945, K. Sokolov and Aleksandr Norov developed a modified feed which allowed disintegrating-link belts to be fed from either side of the receiver. Changes were made to the feed block, saving weight, and a suppressor was added to prevent the breechblock bouncing back from the breech face during the closing stroke. The barrel-attachment system was also revised. This allowed the permissible stoppage rate to decline from eight rounds per thousand for the DShK to less than four per thousand for the DShKM. The first guns were made in Saratov in February 1945, but production is believed to have moved to Kovrov after the end of the war.

Variants
Type 54 A minor Chinese-made variant of the DShKM.
Type 59 This was a Chinese Type 54 with its muzzle brake altered to handle discarding-sabot (APDS) ammunition.

128 *A Chinese-made 12.7mm DShKM machine-gun on a tank-turret mount.*

Medium-support or vehicle machine-gun; Stankoviy Pulemet Goryunova Modernizirovanniy
Made by the Kovrov machine-gun factory
Specification SGM, standard version
Calibre 7.62mm (.30)
Cartridge 7.62x54, rimmed
Operation Gas operated, automatic fire only
Locking system Laterally pivoting bolt
Length 1120mm
Weight 13.65kg
Barrel 720mm, four grooves, right-hand twist
Feed 250-round metallic-link belt
Rate of fire 650±50rds/min
Muzzle velocity 800m/sec

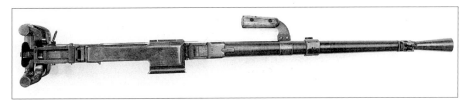

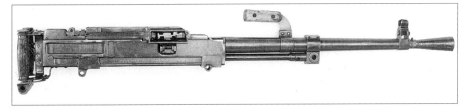

The original version of the SG or SG-43 machine-gun. Note the plain barrel surface and the charging handle placed transversely beneath the spade grips.

The failure of the DS (Degtyarev) heavy machine-gun, which had been adopted in 1939, forced the Soviet authorities to concentrate on production of the venerable 1910-pattern water-cooled Maxim Gun once the Second World War began. However, the Maxim was difficult to make and a simpler design was desperately sought in the face of the wholesale dislocation of manufacturing industry following the German occupation of western Russia.

An ideal solution was found in the work of Petr Goryunov, a one-time pupil of Degtyarev, whose basic design was developed after his premature death in 1943 by his nephew Mikhail Goryunov and Vasiliy Voronkov.

Developed from the prototype GVG of 1940–1 and a series of competitive trials undertaken from May 1942, the SG showed great promise. Operated by gas tapped from the bore to strike a piston in a tube beneath the barrel, the Goryunov was locked by allowing the bolt-carrier

post to cam the tail of the breech-bolt outward into the right wall of the receiver. Tests against an improved DS showed the SG to be simpler and more durable, allowing it to be adopted on 14 May 1943. The gun was ordered into immediate mass production; by the autumn of 1944, 74,000 had been made.

The SG had a detachable barrel weighing about 4.3kg and a folding-leaf backsight on top of the receiver behind the feed mechanism. The front sight could be screwed into its housing to **129**

The improved SGM on its original wheeled mount.

adjust point of impact vertically, the windage adjustment being provided on the backsight. The closed-pocket metal-link belt fed from the left, but the use of rimmed ammunition meant that each cartridge had to be drawn back and down before it could be rammed into the chamber. Combat experience showed that the Goryunov, though it was sturdy, reliable and performed surprisingly well, was also susceptible to case-head separations and other teething troubles.

The wedge-like connection between the detachable barrel and the receiver worked loose too easily, and the integration of the sear and the piston-rod extension was unsatisfactory. After the war ended, therefore, the opportunity was taken to redesign the offending parts, resulting in the SGM. Most SGM machine-guns have fluted barrels, instead of the plain-surface SG pattern, the sear block became a separate component, the charging handle was

moved from an awkward position beneath the backplate to a better location on the right side of the receiver, and a new latch-type barrel lock (eventually accompanied by a special micrometer-type headspace adjustment) was provided.

The SG had been issued on a wheeled mount with a tubular U-shaped trail and a heavy armoured shield. The mount was provided with coarse traverse and coarse/fine elevation adjusters, but, in an emergency, the traverse could be unlocked to allow a 360-degree movement. An anti-aircraft pintle was provided on the tip of the gun-cradle arm. The wheeled mount was eventually replaced by a lightweight tripod designed by Viktor Malinovsky and Aleksandr Sidorenko.

Variants

In addition to Soviet guns, and the Hungarian derivation described below, Goryunov-pattern machine-guns have been made in Czechoslovakia and Poland. These are marked 'vz. 43' and 'Wz. 43' respectively; they are often also found with sights graduated in Arabic numerals, indicating service in countries such as Egypt, Iraq, Iran, Syria or the UAR. Many others have been retrieved from Africa.

SGB This designation was applied to SG machine-guns fitted with an improved barrel lock and dust covers on the feed and ejection ports. It is suspected that these were guns that had been returned for repair during the production life of the SGMB (*see* below).

SGMB A minor variant of the SGM, these late-production guns had dust covers over the feed and ejection ports.

SGMT The success of the SG and SGM machine-guns persuaded the Soviet authorities to introduce a variant to serve tanks and armoured vehicles. The SGMT could be mounted on a buffered cradle, coaxially with the main armament, or in the steering compartment under the control of the driver. Coaxial guns were provided with optical sights, a cartridge-belt support was added and a spent-case bag appeared over the ejection port. The charging system was altered either to a cable or to function by compressed air and a solenoid was added in the trigger system.

Hungarian pattern This gun has been adapted to serve as a GPMG. Though basically an SGM, it has a solid RPD-type butt, a conventional pistol-grip/trigger-guard assembly, and a trapezoidal ejection port. Though the resulting weapon bears a passing resemblance to the PK (Kalashnikov) design, the absence of a cut-out in the butt provides an instantaneous identifying feature.

RP-46

Light-support machine-gun; Rotniy Pulemet Obraztsa 1946g

Made by the Kovrov machine-gun factory

Specification RP-46, standard pattern

Calibre 7.62mm (.30)

Cartridge 7.62x54, rimmed

Operation Gas operated, automatic fire only

Locking system Pivoting flaps set into the bolt

Length 1280mm

Weight 12.95kg with bipod

Barrel 605mm, four grooves, right-hand twist

Feed 200- or 250-round belt

Rate of fire 600±50rds/min

Muzzle velocity 825m/sec with steel-core rifle bullet

This was little more than a belt-fed version of the DPM, described above, intended to give a better fire-support capability than its obsolete pan-feed predecessors. The design work has been credited in the Soviet Press to Petr Polyakov and Aleksey Dubynin, who altered the gas-piston system and provided a new feed block driven by the

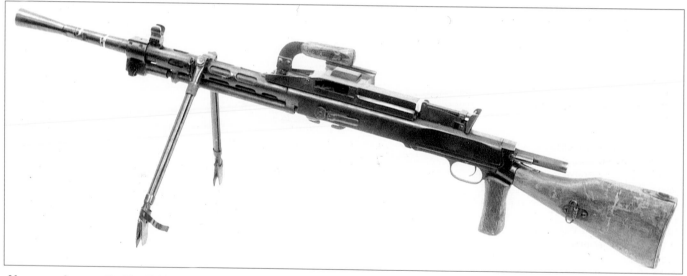

Above and opposite *The 7.62mm RP-46 machine-gun was little more than a belt-feed derivative of the DPM. The resemblance is unmistakable in the design of the receiver and the position of the return spring.*

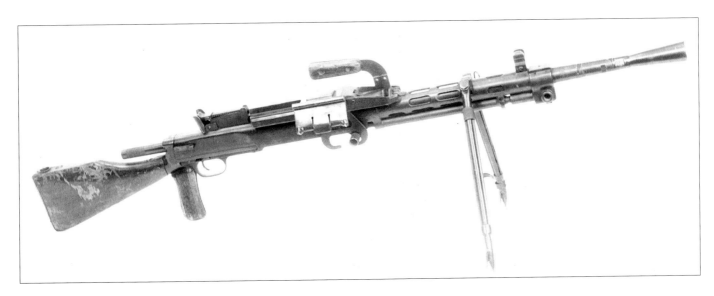

bolt carrier and the charging-handle base – a crude method which worked surprisingly well, particularly as, like virtually all Soviet machine-guns, the RP-46 fired rimmed cartridges which had to be withdrawn backward from the belt before being rammed into the chamber.

The RP-46 had a heavier barrel than the DPM, weighing 3.2kg, but its comparatively light weight restricted fire to about 500 rounds before cooking-off became a real problem. However, a barrel-release catch lay on the left side of the receiver, and the three-position gas-regulator catch engaged in grooves in

the gas block – excepting on the last of the Chinese-made copies, which had a rotary adjuster. The standard pan magazine of forty-seven rounds could be used if the feed cover was changed.

The RP-46 worked well enough, but was about 2.5kg (5.5lb) heavier than the DPM. Though the RP-46 and 500 rounds in belts weighed 10kg less than a DPM and 500 rounds in pan magazines, encouraging progress with light machine-guns chambering the 7.62x39 intermediate cartridge kept production to a minimum.

Variants
Type 58 This was a copy of the RP-46 emanating from the People's Republic of China.
Type 64 A North Korean variant of the RP-46, apparently made only in small numbers.

*Light-support machine-gun; Ruchnoi
Pulemet Degtyareva Modernizirovanniy*
Made by the Kovrov machine-gun
factory and possibly also in Tula
Specification RPD, standard
production version
Calibre 7.62mm (.30)
Cartridge 7.62x39 M43, rimless
Operation Gas operated, automatic fire
only
Locking system Pivoting flaps set into
the bolt
Length 1037mm
Weight 7.1kg (with bipod)
Barrel 520mm, four grooves, right-hand
twist
Feed 100-round metal-link belt
Rate of fire 700±50rds/min
Muzzle velocity 735m/sec

The RPD was the outcome of trials
undertaken during the last few months of
the Second World War with a series of
rival light machine-guns chambered for
the 7.62mm intermediate (M43)
cartridge. Made in small quantities for
trials, the RD-44 was a fixed-barrel belt-
feed design with an integral bipod. Gas
was tapped from a port midway along
the barrel and led back to strike the bolt
134 carrier. This tipped the bolt out of

Top *A Soviet-made RPD, with reciprocating charging handle and the backsight windage
adjustment on the left side.* **Above** *This Chinese-made Type 56-1 light machine-gun
(RPD), made by Factory No.36 in the early 1960s, shows detail differences from the
original Soviet patterns in the design of the gas-port / piston unit and the position of the
fore-end.*

engagement with the receiver and allowed the breech to open.

Adopted in 1953, the perfected RPD had a bulky wooden fore-end instead of the forward pistol grip found on some examples of the RD-44. The receiver bore a considerable resemblance to the DPM/RP-46 design, but the feed block handled a continuous open-pocket metal-link belt contained in a lightweight drum suspended beneath the receiver. Internally, the locking flaps were forced out into their recesses by a wedge on the top of the slide, instead of shoulders on the firing pin. This was an additional mechanical safety feature, as the firing pin could not be struck until the flaps were in place.

The principal saving was weight; an RPD with 300 rounds weighed only 11.3kg, compared with 21.5kg for a DPM. The lack of a quick-change barrel, which greatly restricted sustained-fire capabilities, was regarded as an acceptable penalty for the light weight of the gun. The Soviet designers of the 1940s seem to have considered, with some justification at the time, that detachable barrels almost always meant increased weight.

Though overhauled in recent years by the RPK with its box magazine, which is little more than a heavy-barrelled assault rifle, the RPD has been made in vast quantities. The original guns had a cupped-head gas piston with a spigot-type gas-port; the gas regulator was adjustable. The guns lacked dust covers and had charging handles which reciprocated with the bolt. The windage-adjustment drum on the backsight lay on the right.

The second version had a spigot-type piston and a cupped gas-port, but was otherwise similar to its predecessor; however, the backsight knob was moved to the left. The leaf of the backsight on top of the feed-way cover is graduated to 900m and the post-like front sight can be screwed into the sight block to adjust elevation. The third pattern of the RPD was the same as its predecessor, but had a folding non-reciprocating charging handle and folding dust covers on the feed and ejection ports. The fourth subvariety had an elongated gas cylinder, a friction roller on the piston slide and a buffer built into the butt to prevent the bolt-carrier striking the rear of the receiver on the backward stroke. This and the fifth version, with a folding feed-cover/belt carrier and a multi-piece cleaning rod in a butt trap, are often known as the RPDM. A bracket for the NSP-2 infra-red sight may be attached to the left side of the RPDM receiver.

Variants

Type 56 This Chinese-made gun is virtually identical with the third-pattern Soviet RPD described previously.

Type 56-1 Another of the Chinese guns, this duplicates the fourth-pattern Soviet RPD (RPDM) and can be distinguished largely by the manufacturer's markings on the receiver.

Type 62 Made in the People's Republic of Korea, this is a near duplicate of the Chinese Type 56-1.

General-purpose or vehicle machine-gun; Pulemet Kalashnikova
Made by the Tula small-arms factory
Specification PK
Data for Yugoslav M80 copy of the PKM, from manufacturer's literature, *c.*1985
Calibre 7.62mm (.30)
Cartridge 7.62x54 Soviet, rimless
Operation Gas operated, selective fire
Locking system Rotating bolt
Length 1175mm
Weight 10.0kg with bipod
Barrel 658mm (with flash-hider), four grooves, right-hand twist
Feed 250-round metal-link belt
Rate of fire 650±50rds/min
Muzzle velocity 825m/sec (147-grain bullet)

The first attempts to provide a universal or general-purpose machine-gun in the Soviet Army were made in the late 1940s. Vasiliy Degtyarev offered an adaptation of the RPD, mounted on a light aluminium tripod, whereas Vladimir Silin based his model on the Goryunov. None of the prototypes were acceptable, however, and trials were undertaken in the early 1950s with new gas-operated designs, the most promising being submitted by Mikhail Kalashnikov and by

Top and above *A Soviet-made PKM machine-gun, showing the stamped feed cover and plain barrel.*

a team headed by Grigory Nikitin and Yuri Sokolov.

The operating system and rotating-bolt locking mechanism of the Kalashnikov was based on the AK assault rifle and the SG and the RPD machine-guns; the Nikitin-Sokolov (NS) relied on a slot in the carrier to rotate the bolt and a stud on the bolt to operate the belt-feed pawl. Field trials showed the Kalashnikov to be simpler and more reliable, as the efficiency of the NS feed system declined when it became wet. In 1961, therefore, the Kalashnikov general-purpose machine-gun was adopted and production of the Goryunov pattern ceased.

Operated by tapping propellant gas from the bore and leading it back to rotate the bolt by way of the bolt carrier, the PK was intended to be issued with a bipod, serving as a light-support weapon (PK), or in a tripod-mounted sustained-fire role (PKS). The original guns had heavy barrels weighing about 2.6kg, fluted longitudinally, and a feed cover made from a mixture of stamped and machined parts. The charging handle lay on the right side of the receiver, a safety catch was fitted behind the trigger, and a variable gas regulator was provided. The barrel-latching system was adapted from the perfected SG (Goryunov) type, while the bore and chamber were chromed to reduce the effects of fouling and propellant-gas erosion. Backsights were apparently graduated to 1500m.

Made largely of stampings and pressings to simplify production, the first PK weighed about 9kg. The feed belt was originally a single 250-round strip, but is now made in sections of twenty-five rounds. An 'assault magazine' – little more than a belt box holding 100 rounds – can be attached beneath the PK receiver when required. Published figures indicate that the 100-round box weighs 3.9kg laden, compared with 9.4kg for the 250-round pattern.

Variants

PKM Dating from the mid-1960s, this was an improved version of the PK, with a light plain-surface barrel, a stamped feed cover and a hinged shoulder plate on the heel of the butt. It weighs about 8.4kg.

PKMB This was the vehicle gun in the series, with distinctive spade grips and a butterfly trigger on the backplate instead of the standard butt and pistol grip.

PKMS A tripod-mounted version of the PKM (*see* above). The original tripod mount was replaced in 1969 by an improved Stepanov pattern weighing only 4.5kg – merely 60 per cent of the gun weight – compared with 7.2kg (86 per cent) of the Samozhenkov design. A special bracket allowed a cartridge-belt box to be attached on the march or in battle, and by reducing complexity (the Stepanov tripod had twenty-nine fewer parts than the Samozhenkov type) manufacturing time was reduced by nearly 40 per cent by combining several functions in single components.

PKMT Bearing the same resemblance to the PKT as the PKM does to the PK, this improved tank gun was introduced in the mid-1960s.

PKS The *Stankoviy Pulemet Kalashnikova* designation was associated with PK machine-guns mounted on the Samozhenkov tripod.

PKT Introduced in 1962 to replace the SGMT, specifically for use in tanks (*tankoviy*), this was distinguished by a solenoid firing mechanism, though a mechanical trigger/safety system can be

The PKT is the tank/vehicle derivative of the PK series, usually mounted coaxially with the main gun of a tank or armoured car. The trigger is customarily operated electrically, by way of a solenoid, and a cable-operated charging system may be fitted.

used in an emergency. The PKT has a 722mm barrel, duplicating the ballistics of the SGMT to prevent tank-sights being altered, though the barrel is appreciably heavier and able to sustain fire for longer periods than the Goryunov pattern. Muzzle velocity is 865m/sec. The PKT lacks butt, pistol grip and sights, and has a venturi-type gas regulator to minimise the exhaust of propellant gas into the vehicles. A spring latch added to the gas-piston tube prevents the barrel rotating within the receiver in a bid to preserve accuracy for which the SGMT was renowned. The PKT is, however, much less affected than its predecessor by case-head separations and stoppages are much easier to clear, as the gun can be partly stripped without removing it from its shock-absorbing cradle.

Copies Made by Zavodi Crvena Zastava of Kragujevac, the Yugoslavian M80 is a variant of the PKM with a solid butt instead of the cutaway pattern preferred by the Soviets and the Russians. Used as a light-support weapon or mounted on a 5kg tripod, the M80 may be encountered with a 3x ONS-1 optical sight, which weighs 1130g with its mounting bracket; alternatively, the PN5x80 (j) passive night sight may be fitted, raising weight by about 2.2kg.

Top and above *The Yugoslavian version of the PK is called the M80 and may be mounted on a bipod for use in a light-support role, or on a tripod to enable fire to be sustained. Both the guns shown here are fitted with the 3x ONS-1 optical sight, but may also be encountered with the PN5x80 (j) electro-optical pattern.*

KPV

Heavy-support, aircraft or vehicle machine-gun; Krupnokaliberniy Pulemet Vladimorova
Made by the Kovrov machine-gun factory
Specification KPV, standard pattern
Calibre 14.5mm (.571)
Cartridge 14.5x115, rimless
Operation Gas assisted short-recoil, automatic fire only
Locking system Rotating bolt
Length 2005mm
Weight 49.25kg
Barrel 1345mm, eight grooves, right-hand twist
Feed Metal-link belt
Rate of fire 600±25rds/min
Muzzle velocity 1000m/sec

British and other officers inspect a 14.5mm KPV machine-gun of the Zimbabwean army, mounted on a wheeled ZGU-1. The photograph emphasises the bulk of the KPV, which, considerably more powerful than the .50 M2 Browning, makes an effective anti-aircraft weapon. An array of Yugoslav-made Kalashnikov rifles and an ancient PPS submachine-gun (possibly Chinese-made) are also visible.

This powerful weapon, attributed to Semen Vladimirov, originated when a specification was prepared during the Second World War for a machine-gun chambering the powerful 14.5mm cartridge developed for the PTRD and PTRS anti-tank rifles. Substantially more powerful than the ubiquitous .50-calibre Browning cartridge, firing a bullet capable of piercing 32mm armour-plate at 500m (right-angle impact) compared with only 22mm by the Browning, the Soviet round required a large and heavy gun.

Developed by combining the best features of the experimental 7.62mm SPV and the 20mm APV, the prototype KPV appeared in 1944 but was not perfected until after the Second World War had ended. The KPV operates by allowing the barrel to recoil far enough to allow rollers on each side of the bolt head to run in cam paths on the bolt body, rotating the interrupted-thread locking lugs out of the engagement with the barrel sleeve.

The assistance of a muzzle booster, which diverts part of the propellant gas backward to accelerate barrel recoil, is used to throw the bolt open. A slide attached to the bolt operates the reciprocating feed block, which can be rapidly altered to accept cartridges from either side of the breech. The closed-pocket metal-link belt, made of ten-round sections joined together, is customarily contained in a separate box. A buffer is mounted in the rear of the receiver to prevent the bolt battering the gun at the end of its backward stroke.

The KPV cannot fire if the barrel is either missing or improperly latched, nor if the bolt fails to take a cartridge completely out of the feed. The barrel, which weighs 19.5kg with its jacket, is easily detached. The bore is chromed to extend its useful life, whilst accurate headspace is assured by the method of locking the barrel and bolt into the barrel sleeve.

Variants

PKP Most KPV machine-guns have been mounted in armoured vehicles or on anti-aircraft mounts such as the ZPU-1, ZPU-2, ZPU-4, ZU-2 and ZGU-1 (weighing up to 2 tonnes in the case of the quadruple mount), but their power and performance against lightly armoured and thin-skinned vehicles also makes a useful long-range infantry-support weapon.

Introduced in 1949, the PKP was originally accompanied by the Kharykin mount, resembling a small artillery carriage, which had a split trail and permanently attached wheels. This proved to be too cumbersome and was replaced in 1955 by the Baryshev mount – a lightweight tripod with detachable wheels and, unusually, a spade on the front leg to prevent the gun attempting to rotate up and backward during continuous fire. The Baryshev mount weighs only about 35 per cent of the Kharykin pattern. Infantry guns have a tangent-leaf sight (graduated 200–2000m) on top of the rearward extension of the feed-mechanism housing.

KPVT Intended to be mounted coaxially with the main armament of battle tanks, this is a modified version of the infantry gun with a large-diameter receiver cover, a modified barrel-attachment system and an electromagnetic trigger system. Most guns have a shot counter and a large-diameter sleeve to ensure that spent cases are expelled forward, away from the vehicle compartment; some are charged pneumatically, others may rely on a cable-type retractor.

Pirat This Polish-made variant, a product of Zaklady Metalowe Lucznik of Radom, will be encountered on a specially designed tripod. This enables what is basically an aircraft weapon to serve in a ground role, where it is powerful but undeniably cumbersome.

Type 59 This Chinese-made version of the standard KPV may be found on a variety of wheeled mounts. The Types 56 and 58 were indigenous variants of the ZPU-4 and ZPU-2 respectively, and the Type 75 was essentially a ZPU-1; the Type 75-1 was a derivative of the Type 75 suited to manual or animal-pack transport.

Heavy-support or vehicle machine-gun;
Pulemet Nikitina-Sokolova-Volkova
Apparently made by the Tula small-arms
factory
Specification NSV, infantry version
Calibre 12.7mm (.50)
Cartridge 12.7x108, rimless
Operation Gas operated, automatic fire
only
Locking system Multi-part bolt and lug
system (*see* text)
Length 1560mm
Weight 25kg (plus 18kg for the tripod)
Barrel 1100mm, eight grooves, right-
hand twist
Feed Fifty-round metal-link belt
Rate of fire 750±50rds/min
Muzzle velocity 845m/sec

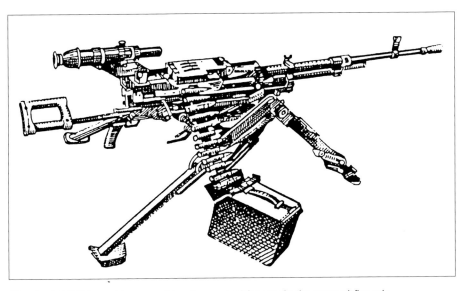

The Soviet NSV machine-gun, tripod-mounted for use in the ground-fire role.

Designed by Grigory Nikitin, Yuri Sokolov
and Vladimir Volkov to replace the ageing
DShKM (q.v.), the NSV originated in 1969
though it was not accepted for service
until 1972.

The gun is gas operated, relying
on a conventional piston/bolt-carrier
assembly to retract the locking wedge
linked with the carrier (some sources say
the bolt is rotated) and allow the breech
to open. A stud on the underside of the
bolt-carrier block operates the feed

mechanism; most unusually, the NSV
retracts the rimless cartridge from the
belt on the recoil stroke, then rams it into
the chamber as the parts return – the
opposite of most modern push-through
systems.

Trials showed that the NSV had many
advantages over its predecessor, being
much lighter than the DShKM. Trials

showed that it was also much more
reliable, easier to make and exhausted
far less propellant gas in confined
spaces such as fortifications or tank
turrets. The 9kg exchangeable barrel is
designed to fire 1000 rounds
continuously before a change is
recommended.

The NSV has been issued for infantry **141**

support on the Stepanov-Baryshev tripod, with a special buffered cradle and an additional sprung buffer in its front leg. In 1976, however, a lightweight Stepanov mount was adopted; this requires the attachment of a conventional mechanical trigger, a pistol grip and a skeletal butt to the rear underside of the machine-gun receiver. Optical, electro-optical or thermal-imaging sights can be attached to a receiver-side bracket when required. Most commonly encountered is the K10-T collimating sight, fitted for anti-aircraft duties.

Variants

Guns of this type have been made in Bulgaria, Poland and Yugoslavia (Serbia) in addition to Russia. NSV machine-guns can also be fitted in bunker or fortification mounts and, paired, in the manually trained Utes-M shipboard mounting. Many will be accompanied by solenoid firing systems and periscope sights.

NSVT Usually encountered on top of Soviet/Russian tank turrets, replacing the obsolescent DShKM, this is often provided with a solenoid-actuated trigger instead of the standard mechanical pattern.

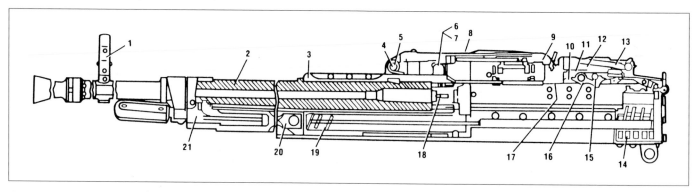

A longitudinal section of the 12.7mm Soviet NSVT machine-gun. **Key: 1** *Front sight,* **2** *Barrel,* **3** *Receiver,* **4** *Feed-tray cover pin,* **5** *Cover spring,* **6** *Feed-tray retaining pin,* **7** *Feed-tray retaining pin washer,* **8** *Feed-tray cover,* **9** *Feed tray,* **10** *Trigger assembly retaining pin,* **11** *Trigger assembly,* **12** *Sight-leaf spring,* **13** *Sight leaf,* **14** *Drive-spring assembly,* **15** *Safety,* **16** *Sear,* **17** *Feed-tray cover catch,* **18** *Breechblock,* **19** *Breechblock carrier,* **20** *Gas-piston retaining screw,* **21** *Gas regulator.*

General-purpose machine-gun; Mitraljez vz. 53 Sarac
Made by Zavodi Crvena Zastava (ZCZ), Kragujevač
Specification Standard light-support pattern
Calibre 7.9mm (.311)
Cartridge 7.9x57, rimless
Operation Recoil operated, automatic fire only
Locking system Lugs on the bolt head engage the receiver walls
Length 1210mm
Weight 12.5kg with bipod

Barrel 560mm, four grooves, right-hand twist
Feed Metal-link belt
Rate of fire 925±125rds/min
Muzzle velocity 715m/sec (heavy-bullet ammunition)

This was a modification of the German MG 42, sharing a similar action, but had lugs on the bolt head instead of rollers. It could be found on a bipod weighing about 1kg, or on a tripod/anti-aircraft adaptor unit weighing 23.7kg. The detachable barrel could be removed through a slot in the right side of the barrel casing. A drum holding a fifty-round belt, which weighed 2.5kg loaded, could be used instead of a continuous feed.

The Yugoslavs have made a variety of light-support weapons based on the ZCZ-made Kalashnikov assault rifles. However, only one version of the original M65 had a detachable barrel, and the fixed-barrel guns are more accurately classed as heavy assault rifles.

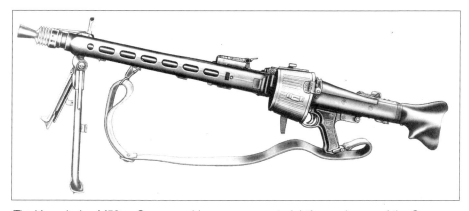

The Yugoslavian M53 or Sarac machine-gun was a straightforward copy of the German MG 42, distinguished by little other than manufacturing details and markings.

Appendix: Machine-gun ammunition

The table gives brief details of the principal cartridges chambered in the machine-guns described in this book. The figures are self-explanatory, except for percentage power in the last column, which relates the energy of each individual cartridge to the 7.62 NATO pattern – showing, for example, that the 5.56x45 cartridge develops a little over half the power of the 7.62x51, whereas .50 Browning is more than five times as powerful.

Cartridge designation	Round overall length (mm)	Rim diameter (mm)	Muzzle velocity (m/sec)	Bullet type and weight (g)	Energy (joules) and percentage power
5.6x45 (.223 Remington)	57.30	9.55	1005	US M193 (3.56)	1,835 (56%)
7.5x54 Mle 29 (French)	76.00	12.25	795	Balle O (9.07)	3,220 (97%)
7.5x55 M11 (Swiss)	77.75	12.60	780	GP 11 (11.34)	3,515 (106%)
7.62x39 M43 (Soviet)	55.70	11.30	710	Ball PS (7.91)	2,030 (61%)
7.62x51 NATO (.308)	69.85	11.95	835	FN SS71 (9.30)	3,305 (100%)
7.62x54R (Russian)	76.70	14.35	820	Ball D (11.98)	4,105 (125%)
7.62x63 (.30-06)	84.35	11.95	840	Ball M2 (9.85)	3,540 (107%)
7.7x56R (.303 British)	77.45	13.45	730	Ball Mk 7 (11.34)	3,080 (93%)
7.9x57 Mauser	80.60	12.00	750	FN Streamline (12.80)	3,670 (111%)
12.7x99 (.50 Browning)	137.80	20.30	860	M2 Ball (46.80)	17,640 (534%)
12.7x108 (Soviet)	146.70	21.65	840	API BZ (47.90)	17,225 (520%)
14.5x115 (Soviet)	155.30	26.90	975	API BS-41 (64.40)	31,205 (944%)